Competition and Governance in African Security Sectors

Integrating U.S. Strategic Objectives

STEPHEN WATTS, ALEXANDER NOYES, GABRIELLE TARINI

Prepared for the Office of the Secretary of Defense
Approved for public release; distribution unlimited

RAND NATIONAL SECURITY RESEARCH DIVISION

For more information on this publication, visit **www.rand.org/t/RRA567-1**.

Published by the RAND Corporation, Santa Monica, Calif.

Library of Congress Cataloging-in-Publication Data is available for this publication.

ISBN: 978-1-9774-0803-7

Cover: MC1 Jeffery Tilghman Williams/U.S. Navy.

About This Report

This report examines U.S. institutional capacity-building (ICB) programs for the security sectors of African partner governments and their potential role in strategic competition. The report outlines a framework for understanding the relationships between ICB and efforts to gain influence among U.S. partner nations and provides initial recommendations for how U.S. policy can better integrate governance and strategic competition objectives in Africa.

In conducting this research, the authors followed Human Subject Protections (HSP) protocols in accordance with the appropriate statutes and U.S. Department of Defense (DoD) regulations governing HSP. Both the authors' and their anonymous sources' views are solely their own and do not represent the official policy or position of DoD or the U.S. government.

RAND National Security Research Division

This research was sponsored by the Office of the Secretary of Defense and conducted within the International Security and Defense Policy Center of the RAND National Security Research Division (NSRD), which operates the RAND National Defense Research Institute (NDRI), a federally funded research and development center sponsored by the Office of the Secretary of Defense, the Joint Staff, the Unified Combatant Commands, the Navy, the Marine Corps, the defense agencies, and the defense intelligence enterprise.

For more information on the RAND International Security and Defense Policy Center, see www.rand.org/nsrd/isdp or contact the director (contact information is provided on the webpage).

Acknowledgments

We are grateful to the leadership of NDRI for their support of this study and especially to Agnes Schaefer and Michael Spirtas, the associate directors of NDRI's Center for International Security and Defense Policy, who oversaw the research. We would also like to thank our peer reviewers, Stephanie Pezard of RAND and Paul Williams of George Washington University, for their insightful comments and suggestions that greatly improved the report. We would also like to thank those who provided informal feedback throughout our research, especially Renanah Miles Joyce.

We owe a particular debt of gratitude to the more than three dozen people we interviewed for this study. Many of these were from the U.S. government, and others were from the governments of African partner nations or from nongovernmental organizations. All of them generously volunteered their time and insights, and this research would not have been possible without them.

Asha Clark provided invaluable research assistance, including a review of Chinese-language literature. Finally, as always, Jordan Bresnahan provided highly efficient administrative support.

Contents

Summary

Institutional capacity-building (ICB) efforts have been shown to be critically important to achieving U.S. security objectives in Africa, yet the role that ICB plays in gaining access and influence remains poorly understood. This topic has taken on new importance now that the United States is emphasizing the threats posed by strategic competition, particularly with China, over those posed by terrorism. Are ICB programs—as part of a broader security sector assistance (SSA) strategy—likely to advance U.S. competition interests in Africa or hinder them—or are they largely irrelevant to competition objectives? Can ICB programs improve security governance while also helping the United States gain influence in Africa?

We use the fairly expansive U.S. government definition of what may be considered ICB, but we are most interested in relatively intensive U.S. support for partner security sector reforms at the institutional and strategic levels. There are three reasons why ICB might serve as an important element of an overall U.S. competition policy in Africa and beyond. First, if ICB is critical to building durable security improvements in fragile states, and if African governments and populations desire such improvements, then the United States is providing a good of potentially considerable value. Moreover, the United States can offer education and training in this field that none of its competitors can. Second, because ICB focuses on higher levels of partners' security establishments than do ordinary train-and-equip programs, which typically focus on more tactical levels, U.S. representatives are often building relationships with more-senior and -powerful partner officials and officers when engaging in ICB. Third, ICB can contribute to U.S. competition goals by helping partners build security institutions that make them more resilient to malign influence or to domestic sources of instability. This can reduce the likelihood that partners will be influenced by U.S. competitors or that partners friendly to the United States will collapse.

On the other hand, there is some reason to worry that ICB efforts might actually undermine U.S. objectives in competition. Some reforms required for successful ICB might be politically painful for U.S. partners. Developing meritocratic recruitment and promotion practices for the military, for instance, might undermine patronage networks that local leaders count on to maintain political support. The same is true with developing anti-corruption measures for procurement procedures. Rationalizing command-and-control structures might inadvertently increase the risk of coups by centralizing power in the hands of top military leadership. An emphasis on respect for certain human rights might be perceived as limiting the government's ability to combat insurgencies. If China (or other competitors) are offering to improve a country's security capacity without such potentially painful reforms, they might be perceived as superior partners.

In this report, we seek to determine under what conditions ICB might further U.S. objectives in competition while simultaneously improving security governance. We provide a framework for understanding the ways in which ICB might help to build U.S. influence in Africa and make it a "preferred partner" for many African states. For simplicity's sake, mechanisms of enhancing U.S. influence through ICB can be reduced to three main pathways: providing *resources* to partners, building *resilience* in partners, and establishing or cultivating *relationships* with partners. For shorthand, we refer to these three pathways as resources, resilience, and relationships.

In this report, we analyze the available evidence related to this framework in two steps. First, we review the literature on SSA and related fields, namely foreign aid, both in Africa and in other developing regions of the world. Second, through both a desk review and interviews with more than three dozen stakeholders, we briefly examine ICB efforts in four cases—Niger, Nigeria, Kenya, and South Sudan—to better understand whether the findings of studies in related fields and other geographic regions appear to apply to the contemporary African context. Without access to data collected systematically over long periods of time, we cannot offer definitive evaluations of the impact of ICB. We can, however, provide a basis for initial recommendations for how U.S. SSA policy can better integrate governance and strategic competition objectives in Africa and potentially beyond. Because of the scale of its current presence and future ambitions in Africa, we focus on strategic competition with China. However, many of the findings and recommendations of this report are applicable to other competitors and to weak and fragile states beyond Africa.

We suggest that ICB, if done right under the right conditions, can pay dividends as a tool of influence. We outline initial recommendations emphasizing the need to prioritize resilience in partners' security sectors, to build relationships through long-term commitments, and to subordinate the transfer of specific military resources to an overarching strategy that emphasizes the first two.

We also recommend specific measures to advance such an approach to ICB. The United States should

- codify and actively socialize a common understanding of ICB across U.S. agencies and departments to rectify the current lack of consensus on what ICB is and what it should be used to accomplish
- create an interagency board or "council" to act as a clearinghouse for ICB programs and integrate them into broader strategies for SSA
- incentivize partner commitment to institutional reforms through selective, graduated SSA, similar to the Millennium Challenge Corporation and with a dedicated line of funding
- build relationships through long-term commitments and intensive in-country cooperation, including through measures such as instituting longer headquarters tours, providing additional resources for U.S. in-country advisors, and making greater use of entities within the U.S. government as well as nongovernmental implementing partners that are able to sustain relationships over several years
- redouble efforts to improve assessment, monitoring, and evaluation, especially of the effects of ICB and other forms of SSA on U.S. influence.

CHAPTER ONE

Introduction

Over the past two decades, the United States has heavily engaged in efforts to build the security capacity of allies and partners to combat terrorism. As the United States' strategic focus shifts from counterterrorism to strategic competition, however, U.S. security sector assistance (SSA) programs must similarly be reconceived.[1] In strategic competition, the extent to which SSA programs build U.S. *influence* might be just as important as their potential to build *capacity*.

In this report, we examine the potential of both U.S. Department of Defense (DoD) and U.S. Department of State (DoS) SSA programs to build U.S. influence in Africa. Because many of the states in this region are fragile and their security sectors under-institutionalized, we focus in particular on the potential of institutional-capacity building (ICB) programs—especially at the ministerial level but also down to the operational level—as a key element of a broader SSA strategy. Because of the scale of its current presence and future ambitions in Africa, we focus on strategic competition with China. Russia also has increasing security ties in Africa, but we focus on China for two reasons. First, Russia is less of a direct competitor than China in many African partner nations that are of strategic importance to the United States, including our four cases. Second, Russia does little to no security cooperation in Africa that could be considered ICB. However,

---

[1] Following Presidential Policy Directive 23, we use the term *security sector assistance* to encompass both U.S. Department of Defense (Title 10) security cooperation (SC) and U.S. Department of State (Title 22) security assistance programs (The White House, *Fact Sheet: U.S. Security Sector Assistance Policy*, Presidential Policy Directive 23, April 5, 2013). Security sector assistance is intended to encompass a range of related terms, including *security cooperation*, *security assistance*, *defense institution-building*, and *institutional capacity-building*.

many of the findings and recommendations of this report are applicable to competitors other than China and to weak and fragile states beyond Africa.

Background

In the years following the September 11th attacks, much of U.S.-provided SSA in Africa was focused on short-term, tactical initiatives to combat terrorism. Until the reforms to DoD security cooperation brought about through the 2017 National Defense Authorization Act (NDAA), many of the legal authorities and funding mechanisms through which DoD worked to build the capacity of allies and partners mandated that DoD programs be focused on immediate, operational concerns rather than efforts to build durable gains in security capacity.

Although it may have been appropriate in the first years after the September 11th attacks, this focus on short-term and tactical-level outcomes came under considerable criticism, for two main reasons. First, previous studies found that weak and fragile states in Africa struggled to sustain the security capacity that the United States had helped to build.[2] Second, and more importantly, many of these states failed to translate any gains in tactical-level security capabilities into progress toward the strategic goals that the United States sought to achieve. A handful of statistical analyses cautioned that there was no evidence that U.S.-provided SSA had helped African partners provide for their own security (understood as either success in reducing violence or gains in broader measures of stability).[3] And some case studies warned that U.S. programs had actually exacerbated instability in some

---

2 See, for instance, Stephen Watts, Kimberly Jackson, Sean Mann, and Stephen Dalzell, *A Developmental Approach to Building Sustainable Security-Sector Capacity in Africa*, Santa Monica, Calif.: RAND Corporation, RR-2048-AFRICOM, 2018.

3 Stephen Watts, Trevor Johnston, Matthew Lane, Sean Mann, Michael J. McNerney, and Andrew Brooks, *Building Security in Africa: An Evaluation of U.S. Security Sector Assistance in Africa from the Cold War to the Present*, Santa Monica, Calif.: RAND Corporation, RR-2447-OSD, 2018; Michael J. McNerney, Angela O'Mahony, Thomas S. Szayna, Derek Eaton, Caroline Baxter, Colin P. Clarke, Emma Cutrufello, Michael McGee, Heather Peterson, Leslie Adrienne Payne, and Calin Trenkov-Wermuth, *Assessing Security Cooperation as a Preventive Tool*, Santa Monica, Calif: RAND Corporation, RR-350-A, 2014.

instances.[4] A number of observers suggested that the United States should prioritize security governance and ICB programs, both to improve the sustainability of capability improvements and to reduce the risk that they would be misused (for instance, to repress political opposition).[5]

ICB efforts can be critically important to achieving certain U.S. security objectives in Africa (such as building durable capacity for counterterrorism operations), but the role that ICB plays in gaining access and influence remains poorly understood. This topic has taken on new importance now that the United States is emphasizing the threats posed by strategic competition over those posed by terrorism.

Are ICB programs (as part of a broader SSA strategy) likely to advance U.S. interests in competition or hinder them—or are they largely irrelevant to competition objectives? These questions become particularly salient when comparing the 2018 *National Defense Strategy* (NDS), and its prioritization of competition, with the 2021 *Interim National Security Strategic Guidance*, which heavily emphasizes the United States' role in defending democracy abroad.[6] Can ICB programs improve security governance (and potentially support democracy) while simultaneously advancing the United States' influence in Africa?

There are three reasons why ICB might serve as an important element of an overall U.S. competition policy in Africa and beyond. First, if ICB is critical to building durable security improvements in fragile states, and if African governments and populations desire such improvements, then the United States is providing a good of potentially considerable value. Moreover, the United States can offer education and training in this field that

---

4 See, for instance, Robert G. Berschinski, *AFRICOM's Dilemma: The "Global War on Terrorism," "Capacity Building," Humanitarianism, and the Future of U.S. Security Policy in Africa*, Carlisle Barracks, Pa.: Strategic Studies Institute, U.S. Army War College, 2007.

5 Alice Hunt Friend, *Civilian Protection Through Civilian Control: An Overlooked Piece of Security Sector Assistance in the Sahel*, Washington, D.C.: Center for Strategic and International Studies, 2020; Querine Hanlon and Richard Shultz, *Prioritizing Security Sector Reform: A New U.S. Approach*, Washington, D.C.: United States Institute of Peace, 2016; Watts et al., 2018.

6 Joseph R. Biden, Jr., *Interim National Security Strategic Guidance*, Washington, D.C.: The White House, March 2021.

none of its competitors can. Second, because ICB focuses on higher levels of partners' security establishments than do ordinary train-and-equip programs, which typically focus on more tactical levels, U.S. representatives are often building relationships with more-senior partner officials and officers when engaging in ICB. Third, ICB can contribute to U.S. competition goals by helping partners build security institutions that make them more resilient to malign influence (such as foreign powers' instigation of coups or weaponization of corruption in the security sector) or to domestic sources of instability. This can reduce the likelihood that partners will be influenced by U.S. competitors or that partners friendly to the United States will collapse.

On the other hand, there is some reason to worry that ICB efforts might actually undermine U.S. objectives in competition. Many reforms required for successful ICB might be politically painful for U.S. partners. Developing meritocratic recruitment and promotion practices, for instance, might undermine patronage networks that local leaders count on to maintain political support.[7] The same is true with developing anti-corruption measures for procurement procedures. Rationalizing command-and-control structures might inadvertently increase the risk of coups by centralizing power in the hands of top military leadership. An emphasis on respect for certain human rights might be perceived as limiting the government's ability to combat insurgencies. If China (or other competitors) are offering to improve a country's security capacity without such potentially painful reforms, they might be perceived as superior partners.

In this report, we seek to determine under what conditions ICB might further U.S. objectives in competition while simultaneously improving security governance. We provide a framework for understanding the ways in which ICB might help to build U.S. influence in Africa and make it a "preferred partner" for many African states. We then analyze the available evidence related to this framework in two steps. First, we review the literature on SSA and related fields, both in Africa and in other developing regions of the world. Second, we provisionally and briefly examine ICB efforts in four cases—Niger, Nigeria, Kenya, and South Sudan—to better under-

[7] Jahara Matisek, "International Competition to Provide Security Force Assistance in Africa: Civil-Military Relations Matter," *PRISM*, Vol. 9, No. 1, 2020.

stand whether the findings of studies in related fields and other geographic regions appear to apply to the contemporary African context.[8] Because the United States has implemented a limited number of intensive ICB programs in Africa, however, and because such programs have seldom if ever been the subject of rigorous evaluations over time, these cases can provide only partial insights. Combined with the review of prior evidence, however, they provide a basis for initial recommendations for how U.S. SSA policy can better integrate governance and strategic competition objectives in Africa and beyond.

The research for this report was conducted both through a desk review and key stakeholder interviews. The desk review encompassed the relevant policy and scholarly literature, including descriptive statistics on key variables. We conducted interviews with approximately three dozen practitioners and analysts from the United States and the African countries of interest, with levels of seniority ranging from ambassadors, generals, and government ministers to defense attachés, desk officers, implementing partners for various ICB programs, and other SSA experts.[9]

Two terms are important to define at the outset: *influence* and *ICB*. We define *influence* as an outcome in which U.S. partners undertake some action—such as supporting U.S. diplomatic initiatives, sharing intelligence with the United States, granting the United States military access, or denying China the same—that they would not have in the absence of U.S. efforts.[10] *ICB* is a relatively new term that builds on the more established fields of security sector reform (also known as security governance) and defense

8 These cases were chosen to represent differing levels of government capacity and two critical regions, the Horn of Africa and the Lake Chad Basin. Further details of case selection are discussed below.

9 A brief appendix at the end of the report provides further details on those interviewed for this research.

10 The U.S. defense community frequently refers to "access and influence" as an objective for U.S.-provided SSA. In this context, *access* typically refers to opportunities for U.S. forces to operate in or transit over a partner nation, subject to the permission of that nation. Under ordinary circumstances, access can be used for cooperative activities such as training or joint exercises. In contingencies, access can be used for mounting operations such as humanitarian assistance, disaster response, noncombatant evacuation operations, or other U.S. military operations.

institution-building. Defense sectors are critical to ICB, yet the term—as outlined by Congress in the 2017 NDAA—is meant to encompass institutional support to nondefense security sectors as well, such as ministries of interior, police, and paramilitary forces. Following official U.S. documents, we define *ICB* as "projects that enhance the capacity of partner nations to exercise responsible civilian control of its national security forces, contribute to collective security, and absorb, apply, and sustain national security capabilities."[11]

The United States uses a variety of tools and programs across the interagency to achieve these ICB goals, including consulting, educating and advising, and exercises. We focus on DoD and DoS ICB programs.[12] Although we use the fairly expansive U.S. government definition of what may be considered ICB, we are most interested in relatively intensive U.S. support for partner reforms at the institutional and strategic levels, rather than the operational levels.

This report proceeds in five main parts. In the remainder of this chapter, we summarize U.S. strategic objectives in Africa and the challenge posed by a China that is increasingly active on the continent in both security and nonsecurity fields. In Chapter Two, we outline a framework for thinking about the relationship between ICB programs and U.S. influence with African partners, and we briefly review the results of prior studies related to this question. In Chapter Three, we turn to case studies to better understand the tensions and opportunities inherent in simultaneously pursuing improved security governance and greater U.S. influence in Africa. In Chapter Four, we synthesize the findings from our desk review and interviews. Finally, in Chapter Five, we discuss the implications of this study and offer policy rec-

---

11 Defense Security Cooperation Agency, "Institutional Capacity Building," undated. This terminology is closely related to previously used terms, such as *defense institution building* (DIB).

12 DoD's main ICB implementer is the Institute for Security Governance (formerly the Defense Institution Reform Initiative), housed at the Defense Security Cooperation Agency, but ICB activities are undertaken by a host of DoD actors, including the combatant commands and components. DoS ICB efforts include the International Military Exchange and Training (IMET) program, the Global Defense Reform Program, and the interagency Security Governance Initiative (SGI) (of which many lines of effort have transitioned to the Africa Bureau in DoS), and others.

ommendations for how the U.S. government and DoD could rethink SSA policies to better integrate and achieve the dual key strategic objectives of competition and improved security governance in Africa.

U.S. Security Sector Assistance Objectives in Africa

U.S. goals in Africa are outlined in several strategic documents. The Biden administration's *Interim National Security Strategic Guidance*, released in March 2021, highlights a series of objectives in Africa, including supporting "development, health security, environmental sustainability, democratic progress, and rule of law."[13] The document also outlines U.S. support to combating climate change and violent extremism, resolving and preventing violent conflict, and assisting Africa's "economic and political independence in the face of undue foreign influence."[14] While the interim guidance heavily emphasizes democracy, this reference to strategic competition in Africa builds on past U.S. strategic documents and policies on the continent, including U.S. Africa Command's (AFRICOM's) 2020 posture statement, the Trump administration's 2018 Africa policy, and the 2018 *National Defense Strategy*. AFRICOM's 2020 posture statement notes the "strategic importance" of Africa and highlights "global power competition" on the continent,[15] and the Trump Administration's 2018 Africa policy was framed primarily around the threat from China and Russia.[16] The 2018 *National Defense Strategy* notes that in Africa the United States "will focus on working by, with, and through local partners and the European Union to . . . limit the malign influence of non-African powers."[17] Despite some critics'

13 Biden, 2021.

14 Biden, 2021.

15 Stephen J. Townsend, "A Secure and Stable Africa Is an Enduring American Interest," statement before the Senate Armed Service Committee, January 30, 2020.

16 Michael Shurkin, "The Good and Bad of the Trump Administration's New Africa Strategy," *The Hill*, December 20, 2018.

17 U.S. Department of Defense, *Summary of the 2018 National Defense Strategy of the United States of America*, Washington, D.C., 2018, p. 10.

concerns about the concept of strategic competition and the ways in which it might distort U.S. policy, and the Biden administration's seemingly wider aperture on Africa, it appears that competition objectives will continue to animate defense policy and SSA for some time to come.[18]

Over the past two decades, U.S. security policy in Africa has largely focused on using a "by, with, and through" approach aimed at building the capacity of African partners to combat terrorism and reduce regional instability. The Congressional Research Service (CRS) estimates that DoD and DoS have allocated more than $6.5 billion in SSA to African partners over the past decade, a level of spending that CRS notes is "high by historic standards for Africa."[19] SSA programs cover a broad array of efforts focused across the tactical, operational, and strategic levels, but the lion's share of U.S. assistance in Africa over the past two decades has focused on short-term, tactical efforts to fight terrorism, as noted above.

Starting in the late 2000s, however, some senior U.S. officials, including former Secretary of Defense M. Robert Gates,[20] began advocating for more attention and resources to be devoted to building the institutional capacity of partners' defense ministries. Writing in 2016, then Deputy Assistant Secretary of Defense for Security Cooperation Thomas Ross asserted that "Institutional capacity-building is the most often neglected element of capability generation, yet it is the element most vital to ensuring enduring capability."[21] Indeed, in the Joint Explanatory Statement accompanying the 2017 NDAA, the Committee of Conference noted that "insufficient attention and resources have been provided for building institutional capacity at higher echelons, particularly the generating force (e.g. those with 'man,

---

[18] See, for instance, Emma Ashford, "Great-Power Competition Is a Recipe for Disaster," *Foreign Policy*, April 1, 2021.

[19] This figure includes DoD and DoS funding (Alexis Arieff, "U.S. Counterterrorism Priorities and Challenges in Africa," statement before the Committee on Oversight and Reform, Subcommittee on National Security, U.S. House of Representatives, December 16, 2019).

[20] Robert M. Gates, "Remarks as Delivered by Secretary of Defense Robert M. Gates at the Nixon Center," February 24, 2010.

[21] Thomas W. Ross, "Enhancing Security Cooperation Effectiveness: A Model for Capability Package Planning," *Joint Force Quarterly*, Vol. 80, 1st quarter 2016, p. 32.

train, and equip' responsibilities) and at the strategic level (e.g. ministerial and general staff levels)."[22] Amid a growing consensus regarding the importance of institutional-level assistance to achieve a variety of U.S. security goals, the 2017 NDAA required that DoD train-and-equip packages include an ICB component, though some observers note that this requirement can just be a box-checking exercise designed to green-light predetermined train-and-equip packages.[23]

Because many African countries' security sectors are under-institutionalized, there are a variety of U.S. ICB programs on the continent, though most of them have small budgets and relatively limited scope in Africa.[24] The United States implements ICB programs across an array of African countries, including Burkina Faso, Cameroon, Chad, Djibouti, Ethiopia, Ghana, Kenya, Mali, Morocco, Niger, Nigeria, Senegal, Somalia, and Tunisia.[25] The type of ICB support the United States provides to African partners is typically tailored to the specific role the partner plays in supporting U.S. objectives on the continent and is targeted at different levels of the partner's security sectors. A forthcoming RAND report found that in recent years, approximately 13–25 percent of U.S. ICB managed by the Defense Security Cooperation Agency (DSCA) takes place in the AFRICOM area of

---

22 U.S. House of Representatives, *Joint Explanatory Statement of the Committee of Conference for the Fiscal Year 2017 National Defense Authorization Act*, Washington, D.C.: U.S. Government Printing Office, 2016.

23 Public Law 114–328, National Defense Authorization Act for Fiscal Year 2017, December 23, 2016; RAND interview with U.S. government ICB implementer, April 2, 2021 (Interview 2); RAND interview with former U.S. Ambassador in Africa, March 26, 2021 (Interview 3).

24 RAND research has documented how various DIB efforts, a subsection of the ICB concept, as noted above, are planned and executed in Africa. Although exact numbers are difficult to determine, this research found that no more than 5 percent of AFRICOM's resources were devoted to DIB-related programs in 2013 and 2014. See Michael J. McNerney, Stuart Johnson, Stephanie Pezard, David Stebbins, Renanah Miles, Angela O'Mahony, Chaoling Feng, and Tim Oliver, *Defense Institution Building in Africa: An Assessment*, Santa Monica, Calif.: RAND Corporation, RR-1232-OSD, 2016.

25 U.S. Africa Command, *Institutional Capacity Support Plans*, June 18, 2020, not available to the general public.

responsibility.[26] Such efforts run the gamut but are largely focused on strategic planning, human resource management, logistics, procurement and acquisition, rule of law and human rights, though some focus areas receive more attention than others.[27]

The Challenge Posed by China

China's Strategic Objectives in Africa

China has significant political and economic interests in Africa. According to recent RAND research, China's overarching objectives in Africa can be grouped into four categories: access to natural resources, trade and market access, international political legitimacy, and security of Chinese nationals and investments.[28] China has historically maintained a hands-off approach to security matters in Africa. However, terrorism, kidnappings, piracy, anti-Chinese protests, and civil unrest have affected China's investments and citizens on the continent and led Beijing to take a more active role in regional security, including the construction of its first overseas military base in Djibouti in 2016.[29] According to one recent report, China seeks a predominant leadership role in global affairs but with a particular focus on Eurasia, the Middle East, and Africa. In Beijing's conception of its role, its "international leadership would be characterized by a reliance on finance,

---

[26] Jefferson P. Marquis, David Thaler, Jennifer D.P. Moroney, Beth Grill, Mary Kate Adgie, and Alexander Noyes, *Department of Defense Institutional Capacity-Building of Foreign Partner Security Forces: An Approach to Analyzing Potential Gaps Between Supply and Demand*, Santa Monica, Calif.: RAND Corporation, forthcoming, p. 24.

[27] U.S. Africa Command, 2020, not available to the general public; RAND interview with four U.S. government ICB implementers, March 26, 2021 (Interview 4).

[28] Andrew Scobell, Bonny Lin, Howard J. Shatz, Michael Johnson, Larry Hanauer, Michael S. Chase, Astrid Stuth Cevallos, Ivan W. Rasmussen, Arthur Chan, Aaron Strong, Eric Warner, and Logan Ma, *At the Dawn of the Belt and Road: China in the Developing World*, Santa Monica, Calif.: RAND Corporation, RR-2273-A, 2018, p. 171.

[29] Max Bearak, "In Strategic Djibouti, a Microcosm of China's Growing Foothold in Africa," *Washington Post*, December 30, 2019.

diplomatic engagement, and security assistance to exercise influence while maintaining a modest overseas military presence."[30]

The Symmetric Challenge: Arms Transfers and Education of African Military Officers

China's security engagements in Africa have largely been transactional, such as ensuring the security of Chinese investments and nationals or providing arms sales and materiel. China is a key player in the African arms market. China's declared foreign policy principle of political noninterference provides African countries with access to weapons regardless of domestic dynamics such human rights abuses. Flexible financing and pricing also make China an attractive supplier of small arms and light weapons. Between 2016 and 2020, according to Stockholm International Peace Research Institute (SIPRI) data—which include only larger weapon systems, not small arms and light weapons—21 sub-Saharan nations received major arms from Beijing, with China accounting for 20 percent of arms imports by states in the subregion, putting China behind Russia (30 percent of imports) but ahead of France (9.5 percent) and the United States (5.4 percent).[31]

Beyond these sorts of transactional interactions, China has also worked to develop relationships with African nations. The People's Liberation Army (PLA), much like the U.S. military, uses professional military education (PME) to cultivate ties with current and future African security leaders.[32] The PLA operates roughly 70 military academies in China, about half

[30] Timothy R. Heath, Derek Grossman, and Asha Clark, *China's Quest for Global Primacy: An Analysis of Chinese International and Defense Strategies to Outcompete the United States*, Santa Monica, Calif.: RAND Corporation, RR-A447-1, 2021.

[31] Pieter D. Wezeman, Alexandra Kuimoca, and Siemon T. Wezeman, *Trends in International Arms Transfers, 2020*, Stockholm International Peace Research Institute, March 21, 2020.

[32] China's 2015 military white paper includes an expansive role for military diplomacy, stating that the PLA will "develop all-round military-to-military relations," including by preserving "traditional friendly military ties with their African, Latin American, and Southern Pacific counterparts" (State Council Information Office of the People's Republic of China, *China's Military Strategy*, May 2015).

of which offer training to foreign military personnel.[33] According to one estimate, approximately 2,000 officers across 40 African countries train in China annually.[34] Unlike the U.S. PME system, African military officers are not typically integrated with their Chinese counterparts but rather taught in separate courses with other international students, typically in English or French.[35] According to one observer, many African partners view this segregated arrangement as inferior to the U.S. approach, in which African officers sit alongside American military officers, learn American doctrine, and build stronger person-to-person relationships.[36]

Chinese PME, unlike that of the United States, does not include content on democratic civilian control of the military or human rights. Some research suggests that China's foreign military education is designed to promote alternatives to Western ideology and to promote China's approach to military management, in which the military is subordinate to the absolute control of the ruling political party. One study documented how a senior African officer recalled Chinese PME curriculum that promoted a narrative of U.S. neo-imperialism in Africa.[37] Another scholar noted that China's strong emphasis on ideology in military training

> is an under-looked yet potent form of ideological influence. . . . Beijing uses this narrative to extend its appeal and outreach across the board, from countries with whom it has strong traditional ties such as Mozambique, Namibia, and Tanzania to traditionally pro-Western ones like Kenya, Liberia, and Senegal.[38]

---

[33] David L. Shambaugh, *China Goes Global: The Partial Power*, Oxford: Oxford University Press, 2013, p. 301.

[34] Paul Nantulya, "China's Strategic Aims in Africa," testimony before the U.S.-China Economic Security Review Commission, May 8, 2020.

[35] John S. Van Oudenaren and Benjamin E. Fisher, "Foreign Military Education as PLA Soft Power," *Parameters*, Vol. 46, No. 4, Winter 2016; RAND interview with former U.S. defense attaché in Africa, March 5, 2018 (Interview 5).

[36] RAND interview with former U.S. defense attaché in Africa, March 5, 2018 (Interview 5).

[37] Van Oudenaren and Fisher, 2106, p. 113.

[38] Nantulya, 2020.

The challenge for U.S. policymakers is therefore two-fold. First, African partners that do not share U.S. priorities such as democratic control of the military and respect for human rights might increasingly turn to Chinese PME—which does not emphasize those values—for support, potentially eroding U.S. relationships and influence on the continent over time. Second, to the extent China sells its military management model to African security leaders and political elite through foreign military training, it might undercut U.S. norms and objectives regarding the loyalty of military forces to the state and population rather than to a particular political party.

The Asymmetric Challenge: Chinese Commercial Investment in Africa

Despite China's increased security footprint, these efforts are dwarfed by the country's economic engagements in Africa. China is sub-Saharan Africa's largest single trading partner.[39] Moreover, sub-Saharan Africa has received substantial economic investment from China over the past decade, much of it in the form of government-to-government loans, which have financed economic and social infrastructure projects, mainly transport, power, telecommunications, and water.[40] Thirty-nine countries in Sub-Saharan Africa have joined China's Belt and Road Initiative.[41]

The ten largest African borrowers from 2015 to 2017 are a varied group of countries: including Nigeria, the Republic of Congo, and Cameroon in West Africa; Angola, South Africa, and Zambia in Southern Africa; Kenya, Uganda, and Ethiopia in East Africa; and Egypt in North Africa.[42] Chinese lending in Africa peaked in 2013; according to Johns Hopkins's China

[39] International Monetary Fund, African Department, *A Rebalancing Act for China and Africa: The Effects of China's Rebalancing on Sub-Saharan Africa's Trade and Growth*, April 2017.

[40] Kevin Acker and Deborah Brautigam, *Twenty Years of Data on China's Africa Lending*, Johns Hopkins School of Advanced International Studies, China Africa Research Initiative, 2021, p. 1.

[41] David Sacks, "Countries in China's Belt and Road Initiative: Who's in and Who's out," Council on Foreign Relations, March 24, 2021.

[42] According to the Johns Hopkins School of Advanced International Studies China Africa Research Initiative Database, as shown in David Dollar, *Understanding China's*

Africa Research Initiative, this decline reflects, among other things, China's concerns about debt sustainability.[43] In addition to lending, Chinese foreign direct investment (FDI) in Africa has increased steadily since 2003, overtaking U.S. FDI flows in 2014.[44] Similarly, China's global foreign aid expenditures have increased globally, with 45 percent of aid going to Africa.[45]

Views on the extent to which Chinese economic investment has generated leverage or influence in Africa vary, and they cannot be generalized across an entire continent. Some observers note that China's push to get countries to join its Belt and Road Initiative is "likely motivated less by a desire to build infrastructure and more by a goal of increasing China's narrative power," and others argue that China's investments are an "effort to stockpile international support for contentious political issues."[46] More cynical views of Chinese investment on the continent include the idea of "debt trap diplomacy," whereby Chinese lending deliberately indebts borrowers to enable China to gain strategic advantages, such as ports or mineral concessions.[47] Other scholars have cautioned against broad claims that Chinese investment could cause African countries to lose control of their national assets, noting that African experiences with the Belt and Road Initiative are heterogenous—some major borrowers have issues with debt sustainability, whereas others have more soundly integrated Chinese loans.[48]

Belt and Road Infrastructure Projects in Africa, Washington, D.C.: Brookings Institution, September 2019.

43 If the outlier of Angola is excluded from the data (Acker and Brautigam, 2021, p. 1).

44 Johns Hopkins School of Advanced International Studies, China Africa Research Initiative, "Data: Chinese Investment in Africa," webpage, 2021b.

45 Johns Hopkins School of Advanced International Studies, China Africa Research Initiative, "Data: Chinese Global Foreign Aid," webpage, 2021a.

46 Sacks, 2021; Eleanor Albert, "China in Africa," Council on Foreign Relations, July 12, 2017.

47 For example, former U.S. Secretary of State Rex Tillerson argued that in Africa, China "encourages dependency using opaque contracts, predatory loan practices, and corrupt deals that mire nations in debt and undercut their sovereignty" (Rex W. Tillerson, remarks, George Mason University, Fairfax, Va., March 6, 2018).

48 Dollar, 2019; see also Deborah Brautigam and Won Kidane, *China, Africa, and Debt Distress: Fact and Fiction About Asset Seizures*, Johns Hopkins China Africa Research Initiative Policy Brief No. 47, 2020.

Other observers point to African governments' agency in successfully using various tools to gain leverage in their "imbalanced ties" with Beijing, and express irritation at American views that China is uniformly taking advantage of African nations.[49]

U.S.-provided SSA does not provide any direct response to Chinese economic initiatives in Africa. Nor should the United States rely solely on SSA and other military instruments in a competition for influence; development assistance and other economic tools are critically important. But to the extent that the United States' African partners value U.S.-provided SSA—and specifically ICB—SSA may be one important factor in the evolving competition in Africa. In the next chapter, we describe exactly how ICB might translate into U.S. influence on the continent.

---

[49] Paul Nantulya, "Reshaping African Agency in China-Africa Relations," Africa Center for Strategic Studies, March 2, 2021; Deborah Brautigam and Meg Rithmire, The Chinese 'Debt Trap' Is a Myth, *The Atlantic*, February 6, 2021.

CHAPTER TWO

Analytic Framework Linking Institutional Capacity-Building and Influence

Influence in strategic competition is one major objective for the United States' SSA in Africa. However, it is unclear to what extent the United States is successful in translating its SSA generally, and ICB specifically, into influence. There are many ways in which ICB programs might enhance the United States' influence in Africa. For simplicity's sake, they can be reduced to three main pathways: *resources*, *resilience*, and *relationships*. In each of the following three sections, we first explain the logic potentially linking ICB to U.S. influence through one of these pathways, then we review prior studies related to that pathway. Because so few studies have directly examined the relationship between ICB and influence, in many cases we must draw inferences from prior analyses of SSA more generally (rather than the narrower field of ICB) and from nonmilitary capacity-building or governance assistance.

Resources

This pathway is perhaps the most straightforward. In it, the United States uses ICB to provide something that African governments value: improved security capacity and/or efficiency. In return, the United States hopes that it can count on its partners to provide things that the United States values, such as support on a diplomatic initiative. This pathway thus represents a *reciprocal* theory of influence. The pathway is not narrowly transactional, in the sense that it need not imply a one-to-one exchange between the United States and its partners. Ideally, in this pathway, partners see the United States as a valuable partner and, over time, choose to reciprocate on matters of concern to the United States.

The most obvious cases in which the United States has exchanged SSA (although not ICB specifically) for concessions from partners involve U.S. military bases. In Djibouti, for instance, the United States provides approximately $63 million annually in exchange for access to Camp Lemonnier.[1] During the Cold War, the United States provided many million dollars' worth of materiel and training to Ethiopia each year in exchange for access to Kagnew Station.[2] Such exchanges are not limited to basing rights, however. The United States' provision of extremely large amounts of SSA annually to Egypt, for instance, was a critical precondition for Egypt's signing of and adherence to the Camp David Accords.

Although ICB is unlikely to be used in such direct, tit-for-tat swaps, there are reasons to believe that ICB might increase U.S. influence in this manner over longer periods of time. In a recent survey, African leaders ranked "peace and justice" as the second-most important of the United Nations' 16 "Sustainable Developments Goals," and ordinary Africans ranked it the most important.[3] To the extent that ICB contributes to this objective by building more effective and accountable militaries, it is reasonable to expect that it would be highly valued by African leaders and populations alike. Moreover, the United States might have a comparative advantage over China and other autocratic competitors when it comes to building institutions. In a recent Afrobarometer poll, nearly one-third of Africans cited the United States as

---

1 Zachary A. Goldfarb, "U.S., Djibouti Reach Agreement to Keep Counterterrorism Base in Horn of Africa nation," *Washington Post*, May 5, 2014.

2 Jefferey A. Lefebvre, *Arms for the Horn: U.S. Security Policy in Ethiopia and Somalia, 1953–1991*, Pittsburgh, Pa.: University of Pittsburgh Press, 1991.

3 Custer, S., M. DiLorenzo, T. Masaki, T. Sethi, and A. Harutyunyan, *Listening to Leaders 2018: Is Development Cooperation Tuned-In or Tone-Deaf?* Williamsburg, Va.: AidData at the College of William & Mary, 2018.

the "best model of development," beating China by nearly ten percentage points and all other states by 20 percentage points or more.[4]

On the other hand, there are a number of reasons why ICB might not yield the reciprocal dividends the United States hopes. As we noted in Chapter One, although ICB can provide many services that partner governments value, it can also involve painful trade-offs for some partners. If the reforms that the United States recommends threaten patronage networks, for instance, gains in military efficacy or efficiency might threaten a leader's political or financial support.[5] Military leaders might also resent programs of instruction that emphasize protections for human rights.[6] Moreover, the military itself might be perceived as a major source of threat, both to the government (in the form of coups) and the population (in the form of abuse and repression).[7] In the long term, ICB can help to alleviate many of these problems. The efficiency gains it can help to realize might free up resources that could be spent to build political support in other ways. Efforts to instill a respect for civilian authority and human rights might change attitudes within and toward the military. But these are likely all longer-term prospects. In the short term, ICB might yield few observable rewards, making it a relatively poor offer in a purely reciprocal relationship, especially compared with Chinese aid that comes with no such pressure for reform.

Although few if any prior studies have examined the relationship between influence and ICB specifically, a number have evaluated the effectiveness of reciprocal approaches to SSA more generally. These studies have yielded somewhat mixed results. On the one hand, some studies have indicated that the United States has successfully used military spending or arms

---

[4] Edem Selormey, "Africans' Perceptions About China: A Sneak Peek from 18 Countries," Afrobarometer, September 3, 2020.

[5] Matisek, 2020.

[6] Many police forces in Africa and elsewhere, for instance, see themselves as guardians of the regime, not the people. They therefore perceive concepts such as community-oriented policing as being "foreign" or "womanly" and not worthy of the state's security forces. See Robert Davis, Nicole Henderson, and Cybele Merrick, "Community Policing: Variations on the Western Model in the Developing World," *Police Practice and Research*, Vol. 4, No. 3, 2003, pp. 295, 297.

[7] Matisek, 2020.

transfers to secure access and basing rights in foreign countries.[8] Analyses of U.S. nonmilitary assistance have come to similar findings. One study, for instance, found a relationship between such assistance and pro-U.S. voting records in the UN General Assembly.[9]

Numerous observers, however, have warned about the limitations of such reciprocal approaches, particularly if there are important differences in interests or values between the United States and its partners. One study of U.S. counterterrorism assistance, for instance, found that it only achieved the desired outcome when local terrorist forces were the recipient state's greatest threat. When local leaders feared other threats more than those posed by terrorists, they redirected U.S. assistance toward targeting these other enemies, and they even had incentives to exaggerate and prolong the terrorist threat to continue to receive U.S. aid (a phenomenon known as *moral hazard*).[10]

Other analysts have warned about dynamics that lead to upward pressure on partners' asking prices for military access or other concessions. One study found that the existence of multiple bidders typically drove up potential host nations' demands for compensation in exchange for military access.[11] Another found that partner nations increased their demands for compensation for U.S. bases when they learned that the United States had paid more for bases in other countries.[12] Studies have found that when the

---

8 Brian Blankenship and Renanah Miles Joyce, "Purchasing Power: U.S. Overseas Defense Spending and Military Statecraft," *Journal of Conflict Resolution*, Vol. 64, Nos. 2–3, 2020; Robert E. Harkavy, *Bases Abroad: The Global Foreign Military Presence*, New York: Oxford University Press for the Stockholm International Peace Research Institute, 1989; Stacie L. Pettyjohn and Jennifer Kavanagh, *Access Granted: Political Challenges to the U.S. Overseas Military Presence, 1945–2014*, Santa Monica, Calif. RAND Corporation, RR-1339-AF, 2016.

9 Axel Dreher, Peter Nunnenkamp, and Rainer Thiele, "Does U.S. Aid Buy UN General Assembly Votes? A Disaggregated Analysis," *Public Choice*, Vol. 136, 2008; T. Y. Wang, "U.S. Foreign Aid and UN Voting: An Analysis of Important Issues," *International Studies Quarterly*, Vol. 43, No. 1, 1999.

10 Andrew Boutton, "U.S. Foreign Aid, Interstate Rivalry, and Incentives for Counterterrorism Cooperation," *Journal of Peace Research*, Vol. 51, No. 6, 2014.

11 Blankenship and Joyce, 2020.

12 Pettyjohn and Kavanagh, 2016.

United States believes a partner is critical for security reasons, it frequently provides aid even if the partner does not behave in ways consistent with U.S. interests.[13] Finally, if the United States provides military resources to a non-democratic government, there is a risk of blowback against the United States if the country ever experiences a democratic transition, as well as reputation costs with other diplomatic partners and U.S. domestic backlash.[14]

In short, if cooperation between the United States and partner nations is based on a reciprocal exchange of U.S. assistance for partner diplomatic support or other favors, it also appears to be relatively short-lived. Cooperation is always at risk if there are changes in the partner's short-term interests or if another power offers more than what the United States is offering.

Resilience

A second means by which ICB might help to achieve U.S. competition goals is building resilience to pressures to misuse the security apparatus for political or economic gain. For the purposes of this analysis, we define *resilience* as the capacity and intent of the security sector to uphold the security of the state and its population from external and internal threats to norms of good governance. In this conception, a resilient security sector is one that refuses to prioritize its own interests or those of a particular leader, party, or subpopulation (such as an ethnic or sectarian group) over the interests of the state or the overall population. Resilience thus represents an *institutional* theory of influence. It might contribute to U.S. competition goals through direct and indirect means.

In the direct path, U.S. efforts to build resilience directly counter competitor efforts to target foreign militaries with the objective of subverting existing governments or liberal norms of governance. Russia, for instance, is widely believed to have attempted to instigate a coup in Montenegro to

---

[13] Patricia L. Sullivan, Brock F. Tessman, and Xiaojun Li, "U.S. Military Aid and Recipient State Cooperation," *Foreign Policy Analysis*, Vol. 7, 2011.

[14] Ely Ratner, "Reaping What You Sow: Democratic Transitions and Foreign Policy Realignment," *Journal of Conflict Resolution*, Vol. 53, No. 3, June 2009.

prevent it from acceding to NATO.[15] Russia has also "weaponized" corruption, including in foreign militaries, as a means of gaining influence.[16] China does not appear to have directly used either of these tools to target militaries in Africa (although it is widely believed to use corruption as a tool of influence with civilian leaders).[17] Beijing has, however, used its education programs for African military officers—programs that educating approximately 2,000 African officers each year—to attempt to promote its party-state model in which the military is subordinate to the ruling political party rather than the state or the population as a whole.[18] ICB programs provided by the United States could strengthen partner-nation institutions, making them more independent and nonpartisan and less prone to coups or corruption, for example.

ICB programs might also serve U.S. competition goals indirectly. When a government that has been friendly with the United States is overthrown (such as in a revolution or civil war), the successor government might turn on the United States. During the Cold War, for example, the U.S.-aligned government of Emperor Haile Selassie in Ethiopia collapsed, bringing to power a military junta that ultimately turned to the Soviet Union for support. To the extent that ICB can help instill norms of good governance and prevent violent changes in leadership—either by increasing security capacity or promoting reforms that alleviate the abuses or failures that give rise to violent challenges—it can help to prevent such diplomatic reversals.

There have been very few rigorous studies of the extent to which U.S.-provided ICB programs promote resilience as defined in this report. Some studies of U.S. military education programs, such as International Military Exchange and Training (IMET), show an association between these programs and improvement in liberal democratic governance or respect for

---

15 Heather A. Conley, *Russian Malign Influence in Montenegro: The Weaponization and Exploitation of History, Religion, and Economics*, Washington, D.C.: Center for Strategic and International Studies, 2019.

16 Karolina MacLachlan, *Corruption as Statecraft: Using Corrupt Practices as Foreign Policy Tools*, Transparency International—Defense and Security, 2019.

17 Salem Solomon and Casey Frechette, "Corruption Is Wasting Chinese Money in Africa," *Foreign Policy*, September 13, 2018.

18 Nantulya, 2020.

human rights.[19] On the other hand, at least one study found an association between these programs and an increased risk of coups.[20] One RAND study of SSA more generally found that, under the right conditions, SSA was associated with a decreased risk of civil wars and similar violent threats. On the other hand the study found that, during the Cold War, the relationship was reversed: U.S.-provided SSA was associated with an *increase* in the incidence of civil wars and insurgencies.[21] Studies of U.S. nonmilitary aid have similarly found that such assistance—and especially aid from the U.S. Agency for International Development's Democracy and Governance accounts—is at least modestly associated with improvements in recipients' quality of democracy—but only in the post–Cold War period.[22]

Overall, prior studies offer some hope that U.S.-provided SSA focused on reforming security sector institutions can indeed promote resilience. It is important to note, however, that the positive results are confined to the post–Cold War period, when great-power competition has been muted (at least until recent years, after the data for these studies had already been collected). And even in this period, gains tend to be incremental, at least in the short term.

---

[19] Carol Atkinson, "Constructivist Implications of Material Power: Military Engagement and the Socialization of States, 1972–2000," *International Studies Quarterly*, Vol. 50, 2006; Tomislav Z. Ruby and Douglas Gibler, "U.S. Professional Military Education and Democratization Abroad," *European Journal of International Relations*, Vol. 16, No. 3, 2010.

[20] Jesse Dillon Savage and Jonathan Caverley, "When Human Capital Threatens the Capitol: Foreign Aid in the Form of Military Training and Coups," *Journal of Peace Research*, Vol. 54, No. 4, 2017.

[21] Watts et al., 2018.

[22] Sarah Blodgett Bermeo, "Aid Is Not Oil: Donor Utility, Heterogeneous Aid, and the Aid-Democratization Relationship," *International Organization*, Vol. 70, No. 1, Winter 2016; Steven E. Finkel, Anibal Perez-Liñan, and Mitchell A. Seligson, "The Effects of U.S. Foreign Assistance on Democracy Building, 1990–2003," *World Politics*, Vol. 59, No. 3, April 2007.

Relationships

Finally, ICB might contribute to U.S. competition goals by building relationships founded on trust and shared values—a *socialization* theory of influence. Socialization involves "the internalization of... prescribed norms and rules. The new norms come to be taken for granted—accepted because they are seen as normal, given 'who we are.'"[23] ICB might be particularly likely to socialize partners, given the frequency of interactions through mechanisms such as embedded U.S. advisors or year-long study at a U.S. military schoolhouse. Moreover, because ICB typically takes place at relatively more senior levels of the military and related institutions, or with military officers who are particularly likely to rise to prominent positions, it might be particularly effective in translating these relationships into important policy changes that are more aligned with the objectives of the United States.

It is particularly challenging to evaluate the extent to which interactions with U.S. military and civilian personnel help to build relationships based on trust and common values. The results of prior studies on resilience likely reflect in part a socialization mechanism, although it is difficult to determine the extent to which socialization explains the observed outcomes. There have been only a handful of studies that have focused specifically on socialization and relationships. One qualitative analysis of states admitted to NATO after the end of the Cold War found evidence for such socialization.[24] A second study found that countries with a higher number of military officers educated by the United States typically had voting patterns at the United Nations that were more aligned with U.S. policies—even when controlling for other potential explanations of those voting patterns.[25] A 2021 study conducted surveys of Liberian military personnel after the United States had played a major role in the reconstitution of the Armed Forces of Liberia following that country's civil war. The study found that more intensive exposure to U.S. training was associated with differences in the way

[23] Alexandra Gheciu, "Security Institutions as Agents of Socialization? NATO and the 'New Europe,'" *International Organization*, Vol. 59, Fall 2005, p. 974.

[24] Gheciu, 2005.

[25] Carla Martinez Machain, "Exporting Influence: U.S. Military Training as Soft Power," *Journal of Conflict Resolution*, 2020.

that forces appeared to think about civil-military relations (although sometimes in unexpected ways).[26]

Although the results of all three studies are complex, it is important to note that the duration and intensity of interactions with foreign personnel usually played a major role in the extent to which socialization occurred; changes in trust and values do not happen without intensive and enduring interaction. These results are also consistent with analyses of foreign influence on democratization processes more generally.[27] Also important is the role of the partner's military in foreign-policy decisionmaking; where the military is not a major player, efforts to build relationships with military officers and other defense personnel may yield few foreign-policy gains.[28]

Conclusion: Common Patterns in the Potential Relationship Between Institutional Capacity-Building and Influence

This discussion highlights a few key points from prior analyses of SSA and from nonmilitary assistance related to capacity-building that seem likely to also apply more specifically to U.S. uses of ICB in the security sector. First, the prior studies found evidence of all three potential pathways for achieving influence. The dynamics, however, were complex, including several unintended second- and third-order effects:

- **Resources:** Reciprocal relationships—in which the United States provides SSA valued by partner nations in return for something the United States values—offer the most immediate path to influence. These relationships, however, succeed only to the extent that the short-term interests of both countries are aligned. Such relationships are prone

[26] Renanah Miles Joyce, "Mixed Messages: Foreign Military Training and Conflict Between Liberal Norms," unpublished manuscript, January 31, 2021.

[27] Steven Levitsky and Lucan A. Way, "Linkage Versus Leverage: Rethinking the International Dimension of Regime Change," *Comparative Politics*, Vol. 38, No. 4, July 2006.

[28] Machain, 2020.

to having U.S. assistance redirected toward purposes the United States does not support, and they are prone to outbidding by U.S. competitors. Moreover, in the case of ICB specifically, U.S. recommendations for reform are not infrequently met with skepticism or suspicion by potential U.S. partners. This latter finding suggests that ICB will only be regarded as a valued resource by a subset of partner nations.
- **Resilience:** ICB can contribute to U.S. goals by helping partners build security institutions that make them more resilient to malign influence (such as weaponized corruption or the instigation of coups) or to domestic sources of instability. Such institutionalized pathways to influence, however, require more time to take effect. They also depend on the willingness of partner nations to undertake relatively major reforms.
- **Relationships:** Finally, ICB can help build enduring relationships based on trust and shared values. This pathway to influence is also typically a long-term one, and it usually is dependent on frequent or intensive contact between U.S. and partner personnel. In what is often considered an economy-of-force theater, such a pathway may be challenging to achieve in Africa. Where successful, however, it promises the most durable forms of influence.

Additionally, a few themes seemed to arise that applied across the three pathways to influence:

- **Long-term engagement:** Regardless of the path to influence the United States chooses, long-term engagement appears critical. If the United States is relying on reciprocal approaches to influence, uncertainty about future levels of U.S. resources reduces U.S. leverage with partners. If the United States is relying on building resilience, it must recognize that institution-building does not occur quickly. And finally, relationships built on trust and common values arise only through extensive interactions over long periods of time.
- **Integration into broader programs:** Outside of cases in which a partner government faces an intense military threat, there are inherent limits to how much U.S. military programs alone are likely to contribute to U.S. influence objectives. Military contributions to resilience are

likely to be circumscribed by the quality of governance of the partner nation. If the United States is betting on relationships, the military is only one part of the government and might not be a major player in key foreign policy decisions.

- **Risk management:** More reciprocal approaches—providing partner governments military resources they want in hopes of foreign-policy alignment with the United States—offer the greatest likelihood of short-term results. But such approaches also appear to provide the most contingent results, with U.S. influence entirely dependent on a short-term alignment of interests. Moreover, such approaches appear to risk "blowback"—jeopardizing U.S. relations with other countries if the resources are provided to highly autocratic or repressive governments that are later overthrown.

Because very few of these studies addressed the effects of ICB directly, however, it is important to determine to what extent the themes identified can help to illuminate the dynamics of ICB in the current African context. To that end, in the next chapter we briefly examine U.S. ICB (and its connections to broader SSA) in four contemporary African cases.

CHAPTER THREE

Case Studies

Because ICB has so infrequently been the subject of rigorous evaluation over time, much of the literature discussed so far offers only indirect insights into the relationship between ICB and competition outcomes. We therefore turn to four case studies of U.S.-provided ICB programs in Africa to better understand whether such programs can yield advantages in strategic competition while also providing needed institutional assistance to African partners. Again, because the available evidence base on U.S. ICB efforts remains scarce—particularly in Nigeria and Kenya—these cases provide only preliminary insights and by necessity rely on interviews with key stakeholders, many of whom are ICB implementers themselves. Therefore, interviews were not always balanced between U.S. and partner nation officials, or between people who contributed directly to the program(s) and outside observers. In some cases, information was so scarce that interviews with program implementers or U.S. officials could not be confirmed through other, non-U.S. (and particularly partner-nation) sources. To mitigate potential bias, we have corroborated all interview information with multiple sources to the extent possible within the scope of this research effort. We also sought to solicit perspectives from different agencies within the U.S. government (many of which have no vested interest in the success of these programs) and from experts and practitioners at nongovernmental organizations.

The four cases—Niger, Nigeria, Kenya, and South Sudan—were selected to represent an under-institutionalized state (Niger and South Sudan) and a relatively stronger state (Nigeria and Kenya) in each of the two African regions of strategic importance to the United States: the Lake Chad Basin and the Horn of Africa (Figure 3.1).

FIGURE 3.1
Map of Case Studies

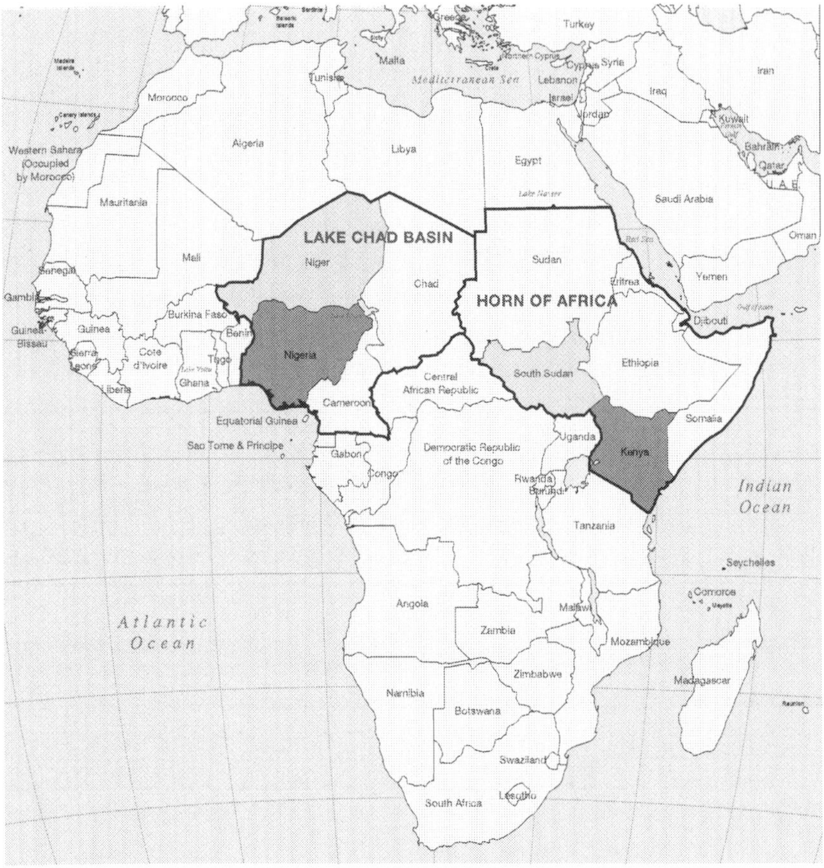

Each of these four countries was a major recipient of U.S. SSA over the past two decades (although nearly all U.S. SSA to South Sudan was terminated in 2014, after the country descended into civil war).[1] The United States conducted relatively intensive ICB programs (beyond simple IMET

[1] In all four cases, these countries received levels of U.S.-provided SSA above the African mean for a period of several years in the post-9/11 era (Security Assistance Monitor, website, 2021—author analysis of data on security aid to sub-Saharan Africa from 2001 to 2020, accessed March 25, 2021).

exchanges) with all four.[2] And all four represent cases in which China provided substantial levels of investment, trade, and/or assistance, arguably providing it some degree of influence.[3] Importantly, the cases were *not* selected to represent "success stories" or even cases in which influence or strategic competition was a primary motive for U.S. assistance. Rather, our goal was to develop a much more complex picture of the ways in which different U.S. goals either supported or potentially competed with one another and the ways in which SSA both succeeded and failed in achieving its stated objectives.

Each of the four cases, or vignettes, is organized around answers to five questions:

- Why did the United States offer SSA? What did it seek to achieve, both operationally and strategically?
- What was the extent and nature of the ICB offered? If it was not widely used, why not?
- What indications of success or failure were apparent in U.S. efforts to build capacity and gain influence?
- How did ICB appear to influence the U.S.-China competition, if at all?

---

2 Among other programs, three of the four were partners in SGI, and the fourth—South Sudan—received considerable U.S. postconflict assistance for the first few years after its independence.

3 China ranks Kenya, for instance, in its highest tier of strategically important countries, and over most of the past two decades Kenya hosted more senior-level defense engagements with China than any other country in Africa besides Angola (Nantulya, 2020). In South Sudan, China has made enormous investments in the hydrocarbon sector. It also deployed an infantry battalion in support of the United Nations Mission in South Sudan (UNMISS)—its first-ever deployment of combat troops in such an operation (International Crisis Group, *China's Foreign Policy Experiment in South Sudan*, July 2017). In Nigeria, the massive import of Chinese goods (which nearly doubled from 2010 to 2016) anchors China's interests in Nigeria. Another salient feature is China's state-directed investment in major infrastructure and industrial projects, many of which are financed by low-interest Chinese loans (Matthew T. Page, *The Intersection of China's Commercial Interests and Nigeria's Conflict Landscape*, Washington, D.C.: United States Institute of Peace, Special Report No. 428, September 2018b). In Niger, Chinese investment is paramount and expanding in the oil and large-scale construction sectors (U.S. Department of State, "2019 Investment Climate Statements: Niger," undated).

- To the extent the United States achieved influence, what appeared to explain this outcome?

Niger

Niger is a key security partner of the United States in West Africa. The country, consistently ranked as of one of the poorest in the world, faces a variety of internal and external security threats. Violent extremist groups operate in the country and region, including Boko Haram, ISIS-West Africa, ISIS-Greater Sahara, and Jamaat Nusrat al-Islam wal-Muslimin. Niger's security sector is under-institutionalized, with a long history of military coups. The country's security sector faces allegations of large-scale corruption and human rights abuses, and unstable civil-military relations remain an enduring problem.[4] The United States provides a range of SSA to Niger at the strategic, operational, and tactical levels. U.S. assistance is aimed at building the country's capacity to counter extremist threats, become more accountable and efficient, and contribute to regional security, namely through the Multinational Joint Task Force (MNJTF) and the G-5 Sahel.[5]

The United States has provided Niger with approximately $240 million in security aid from 2010 to 2019, according to the Security Assistance Monitor.[6] The U.S. military presence in Niger is one of the largest in Africa, and Niger appears to have been the top cumulative recipient of U.S. counterterrorism training and equipment in the Sahel over the past decade, according to the CRS.[7] Several U.S. security assistance programs to Niger could be categorized as ICB. The primary U.S. ICB program in Niger is the joint

4 Alexis Arieff, Kathleen J. McInnis, Lauren Ploch Blanchard, John W. Rollins, Andrew Feickert, and Matthew C. Weed, *Niger Frequently Asked Questions About the October 2017 Attack on U.S. Soldiers*, Washington, D.C.: Congressional Research Service, October 27, 2017.

5 Arieff et. al, "2017.

6 Security Assistance Monitor, "2021, Security Aid: Niger," accessed April 1, 2021.

7 Arieff et al., 2017; Alexis Arieff, "U.S. Counterterrorism Priorities and Challenges in Africa," statement before the Committee on Oversight and Reform, Subcommittee on National Security, U.S. House of Representatives, December 16, 2019.

DoD Title 10 and DoS Title 22 ICB team, which is implemented by DSCA's Institute for Security Governance (ISG) and was stood up in 2015 as part of Niger's participation in the Security Governance Initiative (SGI), a White House interagency effort to improve security governance in six African countries.[8] The Defense Institute of International Legal Studies also runs a program in Niger focused on the law of armed conflict and military justice.[9] Niger is also a member of the DoS's Trans-Sahara Counterterrorism Partnership, which is focused on building partner institutions capable of addressing terrorism in a holistic manner.[10]

The DoD and DoS ICB team works jointly with the Nigerien Ministry of Defense (MoD) and Ministry of Interior (MoI) on a variety of ICB functions aimed at improving the performance of the Nigerien defense and security forces. These areas include strategy, capability-based planning, human and materiel resource management, and budgeting.[11] Publicly available information remains scarce, but U.S. government officials and current and former ICB implementers of Niger's joint ICB team maintain that, although much work remains to be done, their consistent engagements over the past six years have made slow yet significant progress in achieving their objectives and building relationships at high levels within Niger's military and government.[12]

Three current and former members of the joint ICB team in Niger (including one of the authors of this study), wrote in 2020 that the ICB team has made particular progress in the areas of force structure, implementing capability-based and scenario planning, and standing up inter-ministerial structures between the MoD and the MoI.[13] The ICB team helped establish

---

8 The White House, "Fact Sheet: Security Governance Initiative," August 6, 2014.

9 U.S. Africa Command, 2020.

10 U.S. Department of State, "Trans-Sahara Counterterrorism Partnership (TSCTP)," February 14, 2019.

11 U.S. Department of State, *Security Governance Initiative: 2017 Review*, Washington, D.C., 2017.

12 RAND interview with two U.S. government ICB implementers, February 2, 2021 (Interview 1).

13 Ashley Neese-Bybee, Paul Clarke, Alexander Noyes, "Defense Institution Building in Africa," 2020, *Parameters*, Vol. 50, No. 1, Spring 2020.

an internal coordinating body, the Center for Strategic Planning of Forces, "to conduct strategic planning across all security services,"[14] and the ICB team helped to regularly convene a high-level steering committee of Nigerien and U.S. officials to discuss and approve ICB initiatives.[15]

ICB team members argue that four main practices proved to be key to progress: a high-level, full-time project coordinator located in-country to cultivate lasting relationships; the codifying of shared commitments; the fusing of the institutional-level efforts with the operational and tactical; and engaging both the military and the police simultaneously.[16] One U.S. ICB implementer noted the benefits of these efforts, saying: "ICB does have some value from a competition perspective. The relationship is very important, some of the practitioners of ICB [in Niger and elsewhere] have been doing this for 5-6 years or more. . . . [There are] significant second-order effects." Another U.S. ICB implementer maintained that ICB and more traditional forms of train-and-equip assistance were "closely linked" and self-reinforcing, with many ICB efforts intended to assist ongoing operations as well as help the sustainability of U.S. equipment.[17]

Niger's openness to some amount of structural reform has also been important for success. The Nigerien government has a moderate level of dedication to and a strategic interest in making its security apparatus more accountable and institutionally effective. For example, one expert noted that U.S. officials who work with Niger tend to assess that the partner-nation officials are committed at some level politically to a military that is not overly involved in politics or overly abusive toward civilians and are generally open to taking on board suggestions and critiques from their U.S. counterparts.[18]

---

14 U.S. Department of State, *Security Governance Initiative: Annual Review 2018*, Washington, D.C., 2018.

15 U.S. Department of State, 2018.

16 Neese-Bybee, Clarke, and Noyes, 2020.

17 RAND interview with two U.S. government ICB implementers, February 2, 2021 (Interview 1).

18 RAND interview with a nongovernment Africa subject-matter expert, April 24, 2021 (Interview 25).

Despite headway toward achieving some defense management objectives, ICB efforts in Niger have also faced a number of constraints, including a slowdown of work when the U.S. team is not in-country and difficulties in moving the military away from ethnic favoritism and toward meritocratic human resource systems.[19] Moreover, Niger's military remains beset by a host of enduring challenges, including serious abuses, widespread corruption, and tumultuous civil-military relations.[20] Indeed, in March 2021, two days before the country's first democratic transfer of power was set to take place, the presidential guard thwarted an attempted military coup by a Nigerien Air Force officer.[21]

There is limited evidence to suggest that ICB has directly influenced the U.S.-China competition in Niger in any meaningful way. But interviews suggest that U.S. ICB programs have helped to distinguish the United States from China in the security realm and have likely contributed to the United States remaining the preferred security provider in Niger, even compared with the French, who have a long history of security assistance in Niger and the region. One U.S. ICB implementer said, "We're the preferred partner, we adapt to their environment."[22] Another discussed how the United States is well positioned to deliver ICB: "We think about it [ICB] as a way to set ourselves apart from the Chinese, something that we are doing to benefit the partner countries."[23] These comments align with a broader trend among many African militaries. A survey of 742 African security sector professionals from 37 countries conducted by the Africa Center for Strategic Studies found that 27 percent of respondents preferred the United States as training

---

[19] RAND interview with two U.S. government ICB implementers, February 2, 2021 (Interview 1).

[20] RAND interview with two U.S. government ICB implementers, February 2, 2021 (Interview 1).

[21] "Niger: Attack on Presidential Palace an 'Attempted Coup,'" *Al Jazeera*, March 31, 2021.

[22] RAND interview with two U.S. government ICB implementers , February 2, 2021 (Interview 1).

[23] RAND interview with two U.S. government ICB implementers, February 2, 2021 (Interview 1).

partners, followed by the African Union at 21 percent, the United Nations at 15 percent, and the European Union at 9 percent.[24]

While ICB is clearly no panacea for Niger's defense governance challenges, this brief Niger vignette provides preliminary evidence that ICB efforts appear to have contributed to gains in U.S. influence primarily through what we have termed the relationships and, to a lesser extent, the resources pathways. The case demonstrates the importance of partner nation political will, long-term relationships—cultivated and maintained by a well-respected full-time ICB coordinator in-country—and the integration of multiple SSA programs with overarching and reinforcing purposes. Despite these gains, progress has been uneven, incremental, and relatively circumscribed to the area of defense management, with limited evidence of any meaningful changes in other higher-level security governance aims, such as respect for human rights, decreased corruption, or coup propensity.

Nigeria

As Africa's most populous country, largest economy, and leading oil producer, Nigeria is a priority partner of the United States. The United States has provided SSA to Nigeria to strengthen the military's counterterrorism capacity against Boko Haram and ISIS–West Africa, enhance maritime and border security, combat transnational crime, support peacekeeping, and support civilian law enforcement.[25] Nigeria is a substantial beneficiary of U.S. SSA in Africa, receiving approximately $152 million from 2009 to 2020.[26] However, Nigeria's military has a history of coups and has long struggled with professionalism, operational effectiveness, and accountability. Several studies have documented the Nigerian defense sector's persistent problems with leadership and civilian oversight, funding constraints, cor-

[24] Kwesi Aning and Joseph Siegle, *Assessing Attitudes of the Next Generation of African Security Sector Professionals*, Africa Center for Strategic Studies, May 1, 2019.

[25] U.S. Department of State, Bureau of Political-Military Affairs, "U.S. Security Cooperation with Nigeria," March 19, 2021a; Congressional Research Service, *Nigeria: Current Issues and U.S. Policy*, RL33964, updated September 18, 2020, p. 17.

[26] Security Assistance Monitor, 2021, "Nigeria," accessed March 30, 2021.

ruption, equipment and logistics deficits, personnel and training gaps, and human rights abuses.[27]

Given these systemic problems, building the institutional capacity of Nigeria's defense sector has been an objective for U.S. SSA since the country's transition to civilian rule in 1999. At that time, DoS identified military reform as "among the highest priorities" in Nigeria and funded a professionalization program focused on inculcating civilian control of the military and improving the capacity of Nigeria's MoD.[28] More recently, DoD and DoS have funded several SSA programs focused on ICB. Nigeria was selected for SGI in 2014, with programming focused on three institutional-level lines of effort: emergency response and management planning and coordination at the MoI, procurement and acquisition reform at the MoD; and civilian security planning in the Northeast.[29]

Moreover, since 2016 the ISG has advised on sustainment, procurement planning, life cycle costing, forward maintenance, and supply chain issues to Nigeria's MoD, Army, Air Force, and Navy.[30] Since approximately 2011, the Defense Institute of International Legal Studies has provided training to improve the ability of Nigeria's military to conduct operations in compliance with the law of armed conflict.[31] Nigeria has also received approximately $1.1 million through the African Military Education Partnership (AMEP) to support instructor and curriculum development at Nigerian

---

[27] International Crisis Group, *Nigeria: The Challenge of Military Reform*, June 6, 2016; Matthew T. Page, *Camouflaged Cash: How "Security Votes" Fuel Corruption in Nigeria*, Transparency International, May 2018a; Eva Anderson and Matthew T. Page, *Weaponising Transparency: Defense Procurement Reform as a Counterterrorism Strategy in Nigeria*, Transparency International, May 2017.

[28] Despite the reform program having the buy-in of Nigeria's president (Nigeria even shared the cost of the program with the United States), it was vehemently resisted and highly unpopular among senior Nigerian officers, who offered minimal cooperation (U.S. Senate, "The Nigerian Transition and the Future of U.S. Policy," hearing before the Committee on Foreign Relations, November 4, 1999; International Crisis Group, 2016, p. 4).

[29] U.S. Department of State, 2017, p. 9.

[30] U.S. Africa Command, 2020.

[31] Defense Institute of International Legal Studies, annual reports from 2011 to 2017.

military schools, including Nigeria's war college.[32] Nigeria has also received $9.3 million through the Trans-Sahara Counterterrorism Partnership, a DoS program aimed at developing institutions that are "capable of preventing and responding to terrorism in a holistic, long-term manner."[33]

Despite ambitious goals for defense sector reform in Nigeria, gains from U.S. ICB assistance to Nigeria appear to have been limited across all three pathways of influence. In terms of the resources pathway, there is substantial evidence to suggest that Nigeria does not value U.S. ICB in many cases (with some exceptions, discussed below). The United States often views the provision of institutional-level assistance as beneficial for both parties, but Nigeria's defense establishment tends to see this type of assistance as unneeded, intrusive, and an espionage risk.[34] Such resentment is not based entirely on sovereignty concerns; some in Nigeria's defense sector appear to fear that ICB will expose corruption. As several observers noted, as opportunities for corruption have shrunk in other sectors, the continuation of insecurity and terrorism in the country has likely amplified defense-sector corruption and created financial and political incentives for resisting security reform.[35] However, there is some evidence that Nigeria is receptive to ICB that is more narrow in scope. One observer argued that SGI's line of effort on procurement and acquisition reform, which continues to exist today in Nigeria as part of DoD's Title 10 Vertically Integrated Logistics Approach (VILA) program, represents a positive case in which the United States made some headway on addressing defense sector transparency:

> The fact that one of SGI's focus areas—which was agreed upon through a joint process by U.S. and Nigerian officials—approached transpar-

32 U.S. Department of State, Bureau of Political-Military Affairs, 2021a.

33 U.S. Department of State, Bureau of Political-Military Affairs, 2021a.

34 RAND interview with former U.S. official with previous responsibilities for Nigeria, March 22, 2021 (Interview 6); see also International Crisis Group, 2016, pp. 5–6, for a discussion of the Nigerian Army's resistance to ICB in Nigeria in 1999 despite presidential-level buy-in.

35 RAND interview with former U.S. official with previous responsibilities for Nigeria, March 22, 2021 (Interview 6); RAND interview with U.S. government ICB implementer, March 17, 2021 (Interview 7).

> ency and corruption was a big deal. That the U.S. government was talking about plugging holes in defense procurement with senior Nigerian officials in the MOD, Ministry of Interior, and Ministry of Finance was important.[36]

Observers emphasized that VILA is primarily a Nigerian-led effort, and it was Nigerian participants who identified problems with procurement and supply chains; U.S. personnel are primarily facilitators.[37] Another observer noted said that some participants genuinely want to make improvements, though some more-senior officials see reforms as encroaching on their authority and interests.[38] Most significantly, SGI and later VILA's efforts on procurement resulted in the drafting of three procurement policies that, if formally approved by the military, should have a tangible impact on standardizing and professionalizing defense procurement at the institutional level.[39] However, other ICB focus areas beyond defense procurement never got off the ground in Nigeria, in part because of a lack of partner interest and cooperation. For example, according to one observer, Nigeria "knew they needed help on civilian security in the Northeast, but didn't want to take the ICB or provide the access and information we needed. They were more interested in lethal equipment—the Super Tucanos."[40]

It does not appear that ICB in Nigeria has helped to build meaningful and/or long-lasting relationships based on shared values, but ICB has made some progress in facilitating relationships at senior levels on specific issues. U.S. SSA to Nigeria, broadly, has been a point of friction in the bilateral relationship, and there has historically been resentment for periods in which

36 RAND interview with former U.S. government ICB implementer, March 12, 2021 (Interview 8).

37 RAND interview with U.S. government ICB implementer, April 2, 2021 (Interview 2); RAND interview with former U.S. government ICB implementer, April 5, 2021 (Interview 13).

38 RAND interview with U.S. government ICB implementer, April 2, 2021 (Interview 2).

39 RAND interview with U.S. government ICB implementer, April 2, 2021 (Interview 2).

40 RAND interview with U.S. government ICB implementer, March 17, 2021 (Interview 7).

the United States has cut off or conditioned assistance.[41] Despite persistent attempts to improve the bilateral security relationship, engagement on the Nigerian side has been inconsistent and personality-driven, with "periodic bursts of programming when the U.S. finds people within the system who say the right thing."[42] Another interviewee remarked that Nigeria wants U.S. equipment, and the prestige of the war college, but does not necessarily care about deepening the relationship, resulting in a repeated lowering of U.S. standards for the "sake of the relationship."[43]

There is some evidence that SGI and later VILA's sustained, high-level engagement helped the United States to build relationships in Nigeria's MoD, MoI, and President's office, thus gaining insight into institutions which have typically been opaque to U.S. policymakers.[44] For example, VILA employed a respected, retired three-star Nigerian general to generate buy-in for U.S. ICB activities focused on defense procurement. According to several observers, this individual could "open doors that VILA and even the U.S. embassy could not, and ensure that the right people were in the room and were doing the assignments required for the program to progress."[45] A significant obstacle in terms of institutionalizing defense procurement reform is that VILA's programming tends to target lower-level participants (and occasionally those without the requisite acquisitions and procurement experience) rather than senior officials. The rapid turnover of senior Nige-

[41] For example, see Siobhan O'Grady, "Nigeria to Washington: Take Your Military Aid and Shove It," *Foreign Policy*, December 2, 2014; Max Siollun, "No Helicopters for You," *Foreign Policy*, February 3, 2014; Mark Hosenball, "Human Rights Concerns Limit U.S. Intelligence, Military Aid to Nigeria," Reuters, March 13, 2015; "Half of Vehicles Delivered to Nigerian Army by US Govt Faulty," Legit, January 8, 2016.

[42] RAND interview with former U.S. official with previous responsibilities for Nigeria, March 22, 2021 (Interview 6).

[43] RAND interview with two U.S. government Africa subject-matter experts, March 23, 2021 (Interview 9). Through the AMEP program, the United States helps to develop the Nigerian Defense College, which is the U.S. war college equivalent.

[44] RAND interview with former U.S. government ICB implementer, March 12, 2021 (Interview 8).

[45] RAND interview with U.S. government ICB implementer, April 2, 2021 (Interview 2); RAND interview with former U.S. government ICB implementer, March 12, 2021 (Interview 8).

rian military officers also makes it more difficult for U.S. ICB to have a lasting impact at the level that is needed for institutional change.[46]

Finally, there is scant evidence in favor of the resilience pathway in Nigeria. Whether ICB has built security sector resilience to great power interference is likely not applicable in this case, as China has an underdeveloped and transactional approach to security issues in Nigeria. Although China is a leading arms exporter to Nigeria and has considerable commercial investments in the country, it has little interest in building military capacity or risking entanglement in Nigeria's security sector.[47] Thus, China, for its own reasons, has chosen not to target the Nigerian military. There is also very limited evidence that U.S. assistance has helped to build a more resilient, professionalized military. Despite U.S. efforts to provide assistance for defense reforms since 1999, the only instances in which clear progress has been visible are those in which the United States and Nigeria have agreed to target narrow reforms aimed primarily at improving efficiency. Aside from some limited gains in defense procurement and logistics, there is scant evidence that U.S. assistance has resulted in decreased corruption, improved respect for human rights, improved civil-military relations, or any other high-level security-governance objectives.

To conclude, U.S. ICB assistance to Nigeria provides very limited evidence of influence through either the resources or relationships pathway, and almost no evidence through the resilience pathway. Parts of SGI and VILA have been a bright spot in terms of tackling the military's issues with defense procurement and logistics, and building some relationships and goodwill in traditionally opaque Nigerian security institutions, but this work has been more narrowly focused and technical. Higher-level security governance initiatives, which have spanned multiple years and modalities in Nigeria, have not been successful. Nigeria in large part does not feel

---

[46] RAND interview with U.S. government ICB implementer, April 2, 2021 (Interview 2).

[47] Nigeria, the largest arms importer in sub-Saharan Africa from 2014 to 2018, received 35 percent of its arms imports from Russia, 21 percent from China, and 15 percent from the United States (Pieter D. Wezeman, Aude Fleurant, Alexandra Kuimova, Nan Tian, and Siemon T. Wezeman, *Trends in International Arms Transfers, 2018*, Stockholm International Peace Research Institute, 2019). See also Page, 2018b.

any acute need for U.S. ICB assistance, which limits opportunities for the "resources" pathway. There are strong structural factors that disincentivize reforms, making the resilience path improbable.

Kenya

The United States and Kenya have an extended history of close relations and security cooperation. Building on a strong relationship formed during the Cold War, the United States increased SSA to fight terrorism in the country and region after the 1998 U.S. Embassy bombing in Nairobi. Recent U.S. SSA has focused on supporting Kenya's deployment to the African Union Mission in Somalia (AMISOM). The Kenyan military is one of the most institutionalized and capable in Africa, although it has faced allegations of human rights abuses and large-scale corruption.[48] In contrast to neighboring countries, Kenya has escaped recurrent military coups, with the military remaining under civilian control since independence in 1960 (although there was an unsuccessful military coup attempt in 1982).

The United States has provided Kenya with approximately $589 million in SSA from 2010 to 2020.[49] According to the CRS, "Kenya ranks among the top U.S. foreign aid recipients globally and is one of the largest African recipients of U.S. counterterrorism assistance."[50] Over the past decade, Kenya has been one of the top African recipients of cumulative DoD global train and equip assistance over the past decade."[51] Kenya also sends a sub-

---

[48] U.S. Department of Defense, Office of the Inspector General, *Evaluation of Department of Defense Efforts to Build Counterterrorism and Stability Operations Capacity of Foreign Military Forces with Section 1206/2282 Funding*, Washington, D.C., DODIG-2017-099_1206, July 2017; Lauren Ploch Blanchard, 2020, *Kenya*, Washington, D.C.: Congressional Research Service, IF10168, 2020; Narrelle Gilchrist and Norman Eisen, *Corruption and Terrorism: The Case of Kenya*, Washington, D.C.: Brookings Institution, 2019.

[49] Security Assistance Monitor, 2021, "Security Assistance: Kenya," accessed April 1, 2021.

[50] Blanchard, 2020.

[51] Tomas F. Husted, Alexis Arieff, Lauren Ploch Blanchard, and Nicolas Cook, *U.S. Assistance to Sub-Saharan Africa: An Overview*, Washington, D.C.: Congressional

stantial number of its security forces to be trained by the United States, with approximately 3,460 Kenyan students participating in U.S. training programs over the past decade.[52]

There is a wide breadth of U.S. ICB programs in Kenya. According to one U.S. ICB implementer, ICB in Kenya is a priority for the United States because of, among other things, the country's central role in AMISOM.[53] One of the most intensive ICB programs in Kenya is the VILA program, which is implemented by DSCA's ISG (RAND has a lead implementer role, although none of the authors are involved). ISG also supports several other ICB programs in Kenya, including the development of acquisitions and maintenance processes for the Kenyan Air Force, civilian workforce professionalization at Kenya's MoD, and maritime capability development.[54] According to one U.S. official, ICB efforts in Kenya's maritime domain are nascent but represent a priority for planners in the strategic competition space.[55] ISG plans to work with the Kenyan Defense Forces (KDF) on the development of a national maritime strategy and support the alignment of the relevant ministries in the maritime domain.[56] Kenya will also get a U.S. Ministry of Defense Advisor in fiscal year 2021, who will be solely focused on developing the institutional capacity of Kenya's Coast Guard.[57]

Kenya was also selected as an SGI country in 2014, with programming implemented by a variety of U.S. government agencies and departments, including the U.S. Department of Homeland Security and the U.S. Depart-

Research Service, R46368, May 20, 2020.

[52] Security Assistance Monitor, 2021, "Foreign Military Training: Kenya," accessed April 1, 2021.

[53] RAND interview with former U.S. defense attaché in Africa, March 5, 2021 (Interview 5).

[54] U.S. Africa Command, 2020.

[55] RAND interview with U.S. embassy official, April 16, 2021 (Interview 10).

[56] RAND interview with U.S. embassy official, April 16, 2021 (Interview 10).

[57] Kenya's U.S. Ministry of Defense Advisor is funded for fiscal year 2021 (RAND interview with U.S. embassy official, April 16, 2021 [Interview 10]; U.S. Africa Command, 2020).

ment of Justice.[58] DoS also supports ICB in Kenya, mostly notably through its relationship with Kenya's National Defense College, where Title 22 funds are currently supporting an instructor to help with curriculum development, institutional development, and the creation of a $10 million Center for Strategic and Security Studies that will service as a regional hub for those activities.[59]

The VILA program in Kenya aims to improve the institutional capacity of the KDF, with an emphasis on sustaining expeditionary forces in Somalia. The program has four main lines of effort: inventory management, distribution, maintenance management, and procurement. Several ICB implementers and U.S. government officials with knowledge of the VILA program maintained that—despite a slow start and delays because of COVID-19—the program has made some progress, with partner buy-in and recognition that ICB can produce tangible improvements.[60] One ICB implementer noted: "We have moved the needle in terms of how they think about ERP systems [enterprise resource planning inventory management] and logistics enterprise management."[61] Another U.S. official argued that VILA is "a good news story that is impacting the path of their institutions," noting that "the chief of logistics for the KDF and the service chiefs are personally involved in VILA."[62]

Kenya's SGI efforts largely focused on improving border security with Somalia, police human resource management, and the administration of justice. A cross-cutting theme in SGI's Kenya engagements was countering violent extremism.[63] The available evidence on the results of SGI-Kenya paints a mixed picture, with some observers noting movement on relationships and others suggesting that the Kenyans were not serious about genu-

58 U.S. Department of State, 2017, p. 6.

59 RAND interview with U.S. embassy official, April 16, 2021 (Interview 10).

60 RAND interview with two U.S. government ICB implementers, February 17, 2021 (Interview 20).

61 RAND interview with two U.S. government ICB implementers, February 17, 2021 (Interview 20).

62 RAND interview with U.S. embassy official, April 16, 2021 (Interview 10).

63 U.S. Department of State, 2017, p. 6.

ine institutional reform, particularly within the police.[64] On one hand, a U.S. official noted that the consultative approach of SGI-Kenya paid dividends on the relationships front, saying "it's hard to know long-term what the impact is, but . . . they trust us more and turn to us more because they believe we are approaching them in good faith."[65] On the other hand, a nongovernment Africa expert with knowledge of SGI-Kenya noted that the Kenyan government "wanted public relations, a better message, not real institutional reform."[66]

Other enduring challenges faced by U.S. ICB programs include a lack of follow-through when not in-country, difficulty forging close informal working relationships, and differing levels of political will.[67] For example, one U.S. official noted that civilian workforce professionalization at MoD is supported by the KDF in principle but not in practice because of the significant political stakes involved: "The political will for this ICB effort is not there because there is a cost to uniformed military personnel. With a stronger civilian workforce, they could lose fiscal controls and positional power, and would no longer be the only entity with institutional knowledge of the MoD."[68] Moreover, the results of more traditional kinds of U.S. SSA in Kenya, which account for the vast majority of U.S. spending, are also mixed. Several studies point to numerous shortfalls and unintended consequences of such U.S. assistance to Kenya.[69] Interviews with U.S. officials

---

64 RAND interview with three U.S. government Africa subject-matter experts, February 17, 2021 (Interview 12); RAND interview with two nongovernment Africa subject-matter experts, February 11, 2021 (Interview 11).

65 RAND interview with U.S. State Department official with previous responsibilities for South Sudan and Kenya, February 18, 2021 (Interview 16).

66 RAND interview with two nongovernment Africa subject-matter experts, February 11, 2021 (Interview 11).

67 RAND interview with two nongovernment Africa subject-matter experts, February 11, 2021 (Interview 11); RAND interview with two U.S. government ICB implementers, February 17, 2021 (Interview 20); RAND interview with U.S. State Department official with previous responsibilities for South Sudan and Kenya, February 18, 2021 (Interview 16).

68 RAND Interview with U.S. embassy official, April 16, 2021 (Interview 10).

69 Marco Jowell, "The Unintended Consequences of Foreign Military Assistance in Africa: An Analysis of Peacekeeping Training in Kenya," *Journal of Eastern African*

also revealed uneven results of U.S. SSA writ large, yet several interviewees made the case for a greater emphasis on ICB-type engagement to help stem abuses, stay engaged, and cultivate relationships.[70]

The extent to which ICB has directly influenced the U.S.-China competition in Kenya remains unclear, but interviews suggested that a variety of SSA efforts, including ICB, have contributed to the United States remaining the security provider of choice. A former senior U.S. official in Kenya noted that the Kenyans think "of us as very good partners, the Kenyans like U.S. military training, they prefer us over any other provider, they want to go to U.S. military schools and interact at high levels."[71] A former Kenyan military official noted the importance of mutual respect and shared interests with the United States, highlighting how jointly developed after-action reviews helped to forge agreed upon objectives: "It wasn't one side telling the other what to do, but agreeing together."[72] Another U.S. official rejected the idea that U.S. ICB pushed Kenya closer to China, noting that "the United States is providing mostly 'carrot' at this point and not much 'stick.' . . . While a few of the programs may not have the impact we had hoped, they are not pushing Kenya towards China."[73] The same official noted that SSA is the "essential element" of the U.S.-Kenya bilateral relationship and helps to facilitate the conditions for closer cooperation and alignment in other areas, such as trade and humanitarian assistance.[74]

This brief Kenya vignette suggests that, despite mixed results, ICB initiatives do appear to have contributed to some gains regarding influence, mainly in the relationships and resources pathways. The case also shows the

Studies, Vol. 12, No. 1, 2018; Gilchrist and Eisen, 2019.

[70] RAND interview with U.S. State Department official with previous responsibilities for South Sudan and Kenya, February 18, 2021 (Interview 16); RAND interview with three U.S. government Africa subject-matter experts, February 17, 2021 (Interview 12).

[71] RAND interview with former U.S. ambassador in Africa, March 2, 2021 (Interview 14).

[72] RAND interview with former Kenyan military official, March 5, 2021 (Interview 15).

[73] RAND interview with U.S. embassy official, April 16, 2021 (Interview 10).

[74] RAND interview with U.S. embassy official, April 16, 2021 (Interview 10).

criticality of political will, continuity of effort, demonstrating tangible utility, mutual respect, and jointly codified objectives.

South Sudan

Following years of bloody civil war, the Sudanese government in Khartoum and the Sudan People's Liberation Movement (SPLM) signed the Comprehensive Peace Agreement in 2005. This agreement laid out a six-year transition process, culminating in a referendum on independence and the recognition of South Sudan's sovereignty in 2011. Building a formal security sector was a pressing priority for the newborn state, as it had large numbers of organized armed groups and no formal institutions with which to provide security.

The United States provided enormous amounts of funding—ultimately totaling somewhere in the vicinity of a half-billion dollars—toward this goal. U.S. assistance in this period included some initiatives targeted toward very basic needs of the Sudan People's Liberation Army (SPLA) and others that could be considered ICB. The former category included basic skills training for all general officers and senior instructors, tactical-level training, provision of essential equipment, and support for medical services. The latter included the creation of a noncommissioned officer academy, development of a logistics and sustainment center, and—perhaps most importantly—embedded advisors that provided advice on a wide range of essential institutional functions.[75]

In December 2013, however, a crisis between factions within the SPLM triggered renewed violence in South Sudan. Fighting broke out between different elements within the SPLA, which quickly disintegrated along factional lines. As a result of the violence, in 2014, the United States terminated all SSA to the country.[76]

75 Richard Rands, "In Need of Review: SPLA Transformation in 2006–10 and Beyond," *Small Arms Survey*, Graduate Institute of International and Development Studies, Geneva, 2010.

76 Some minor exceptions exist, such as U.S. funding for advisors to support oversight mechanisms designed to reduce abuses.

Despite the United States' immense investment in South Sudan, its programs for the country—both SSA generally and ICB specifically—are widely considered failures. In large part, this outcome can be attributed to the opposition of the South Sudanese political leadership, which was never committed to reform and indeed often actively resisted it. According to one observer, "To keep Western governments' support [for its independence], the government approved and signed up to programs they never intended to implement."[77] In particular, the government found threatening any reforms intended to downsize a military that was bloated out of all proportion to South Sudan's size or to break up the command structures of the organized armed groups that had been incorporated into the military.[78] Two DoS officials provided a more detailed explanation of these programs' failure:

> Despite some tangible progress, a number of challenges stymied the overall military professionalization and DIB [defense institution-building] efforts for South Sudan. These included: 1) a lack of sufficient South Sudanese buy-in as indicated by a lack of resources invested in the sustainment of the force; 2) a lack of coherence with the wider budget and immature public financial management; 3) the inability of leaders to delegate responsibilities; 4) the lack of a human resource management system to strategically vet, develop, and employ personnel; 5) an entrenched antagonism to civilian control, even from the Ministry of Defense; and 6) the preoccupation of South Sudanese leadership with ongoing conflicts and other political priorities.[79]

Could the United States have achieved better outcomes despite the political context? Some critics of the U.S. approach contend that the United States should have made most or all of its SSA contingent on South Sudan's progress in developing an inclusive and truly integrated military loyal to the

77 Casie Copeland, *Dancing in the Dark: Divergent Approaches to Improving Security and Justice in South Sudan*, The Hague: Clingendael Institute, 2015.

78 Lesley Anne Warner, "The Disintegration of the Military Integration Process in South Sudan (2006–2013)," *Stability: International Journal of Security and Development*, Vol. 5, No. 1, 2016.

79 Julie E. Chalfin and Linda Thomas Greenfield, "The Security Governance Initiative," *PRISM*, May 2017.

state and population over political factions or identity groups. One U.S. government official heavily involved in SSA programs at the time observed, "It's critical to engage with the political leadership, not just the military. Unfortunately, we only had a mandate to work with the military."[80] Another recalled that "there was a huge amount of work being done on a technical level . . . in South Sudan before December 2013. We were using a standardized toolkit. But we did not address the political enabling environment" that ultimately led to renewed violence.[81]

Although the United States and other international actors sometimes helped to mediate ceasefires or support disarmament, demobilization, and reintegration initiatives, "there was limited foreign support to the military integration process. Consequently, efforts by the international community to transform South Sudan's security sector were built on the unsound foundation of a fragmented military."[82] Indeed, because members of the SPLA were loyal to individual leaders rather than the state or population as a whole, U.S. assistance—much of which was focused on helping the SPLA achieve operational and tactical proficiency—might have exacerbated that fragmentation and might have solidified the role of the SPLM and ethnic groups that dominated the leadership structure of the military.[83] Although it is not clear that even the best-conceived U.S. SSA program could have prevented South Sudan's return to violence, a more promising approach "would have been to identify individuals in leadership positions throughout the military with a sincere interest in reform."[84]

Although the SPLA as constituted at the time collapsed, U.S.-provided SSA programs from before 2014 had some impact. Some of the U.S. government officials involved in these programs believed that they helped to

---

80 RAND interview with a U.S. State Department official with previous responsibilities for South Sudan and Kenya, February 18, 2021 (Interview 16).

81 RAND interview with a U.S. government official with previous responsibilities for South Sudan, February 12, 2021 (Interview 17).

82 Warner, 2016.

83 RAND interview with former South Sudanese government official, February 25, 2021 (Interview 18).

84 RAND interview with a U.S. State Department official with previous responsibilities for South Sudan, February 12, 2021 (Interview 17).

develop good relationships between the United States and many of the generals with which the United States collaborated, although these were seldom among the top leaders in the country.[85] Overall, however, U.S. relations with the South Sudanese government deteriorated as the United States placed pressure on it to end abuses and engage in negotiations to end the violence.[86] This tension, in turn, created opportunities for China to expand its influence in the country. In the years after the United States terminated nearly all of its SSA to South Sudan and placed pressure on the government to reach a political settlement with opposition groups, the Juba government often saw China as a more reliable and less demanding partner.[87]

In terms of the framework provided earlier in this report, U.S. programs failed to build resilience in the SPLA. Indeed, some critics contend that U.S. ICB programs were too technical in their focus, and by setting aside the broader political context, they might have actually aggravated underlying tensions. Other observers contend that, absent a will to reform among key SPLM leaders, there was little the United States could have realistically accomplished regardless of how it structured its ICB programs. Whatever the reason for the failure to build resilience in the SPLA, the consequence was that the other two pathways to U.S. influence—resources and relationships—were also hamstrung. After violence resumed in December 2013, the United States had no choice but to terminate its SSA to the country, eliminating any influence it might have achieved through the provision of resources. And the pressure that the United States placed on SPLM leaders to accommodate the opposition after conflict broke out weakened many of the relationships the United States had hoped to build. In the end, the failure to build resilience led to a broader failure of U.S. efforts to gain influence.

---

[85] RAND interview with a U.S. State Department official with previous responsibilities for South Sudan, February 12, 2021 (Interview 21).

[86] RAND interview with a U.S. government official with previous responsibilities for South Sudan and Kenya, February 18, 2021 (Interview 16).

[87] RAND interview with former South Sudanese government official, February 25, 2021 (Interview 18); International Crisis Group, 2017.

Conclusion: Provisional Lessons from Four African Cases

The four case vignettes included in this study—Niger, Nigeria, Kenya, and South Sudan—provide some preliminary insights into the potential benefits and challenges of using ICB as a tool of strategic competition in Africa. Very little, if any, of the ICB programs we examined in these four cases appear to have been explicitly linked to a competition framework. The large majority of them were focused on technical reforms narrowly related to logistics and sustainment goals rather than to a broader reform agenda. Overall, the cases yielded mixed results. In Niger and Kenya, ICB programs appear to have achieved at least modest gains—and in some cases, more far-reaching ones—in both capacity-building and U.S. influence. Nigeria, on the other hand, has seen very few such gains and some indications that U.S. suggestions for reform in the defense sector have aggravated tensions in the relationship, although there were isolated instances of improved relations. In stark contrast to capacity-building efforts in other postconflict countries, such as Liberia or Sierra Leone, the South Sudan case was an almost unmitigated failure. Overall, the cases suggest that ICB can, under certain circumstances, contribute to competition goals, although they also demonstrated the considerable challenges involved.

The cases also offered important insights into the three pathways to influence outlined earlier in the report:

- **Resources:** In two of our cases, ICB appeared to offer U.S. partners capability gains that they valued. In Kenya, our research suggests that the KDF values ICB, including its collaborative approach based on shared interests and partner priorities, and that this type of assistance has contributed to the United States remaining preferred partner. Our research also found that ICB was valued in Niger, with the partner government dedicating high-level and enduring attention to ICB. In consultation with the U.S. ICB team, Niger established an internal coordinating body, the Center for Strategic Planning of Forces, and regularly convened a senior-level steering committee comprised of both Nigerien and U.S officials.[88] In Nigeria and South Sudan, on the other hand, key leaders often responded to U.S. initiatives with suspicion.

- **Resilience:** In all four of our cases, although to a lesser extent in Niger, African partners were highly resistant to more far-reaching reforms in their security sectors, such as broad efforts to reduce corruption, improve civilian oversight of the military, improve respect for human rights among the security services, make the security services more representative of the full population of the country, and so on. ICB programs might have contributed to resilience in lesser ways—for instance, by ensuring that partner military personnel had the functioning equipment necessary to do their work, which in turn can reduce the risk of mutinies or petty corruption to meet the rank-and-files' basic needs.[89] For the most part, however, this pathway to achieving U.S. competition objectives was thwarted by a lack of partner appetite for major reform.
- **Relationships:** Our research suggests that ICB can often lead to good working relationships between key U.S. and partner-nation officials, though the extent to which ICB contributed to broader state-to-state relationships based on goodwill, trust, and/or shared values is more ambiguous. In Niger, for instance, the focus of SGI in cultivating lasting relationships through a high-level U.S. coordinator has helped to distinguish the United States from other security providers and has likely contributed to the United States remaining preferred partner. Even in Nigeria, where the United States has struggled to build relationships and SSA has at times been a source of tension, ICB programs had some limited success at building relationships within traditionally opaque Nigerian security institutions by obtaining some degree of buy-in for defense procurement reform. In South Sudan, on the other hand, although there is evidence that U.S. ICB efforts generated goodwill with many individual military officers, U.S. demands for reform

88 U.S. Department of State, 2018.

89 One U.S. official noted that ICB's contribution in this way should not be underestimated. In Mali, for example, the failure of the defense headquarters to logistically support troops in the country's north contributed to the 2012 mutiny turned coup (RAND interview with U.S. DoD official, April 20, 2021 [Interview 24]).

in the dysfunctional South Sudanese security sector contributed to strained relations with the Juba government.

CHAPTER FOUR

Synthesis of Findings

We have suggested three pathways by which ICB may contribute to U.S. influence in Africa, and we have briefly examined them in the context of (1) prior findings from related analyses of SSA and nonmilitary capacity-building efforts and (2) the U.S. practice of ICB in four African countries. In this chapter, we synthesize findings from both types of evidence, as well as from our interviews more broadly with U.S. and African government officials, military officers, and nongovernmental experts.

The Current U.S. Practice of Institutional Capacity-Building in Africa

Recent years have seen a burgeoning U.S. interest in ICB in Africa. For the most part, however, this interest has not been informed by a common understanding of what ICB is, what it should be used for, and how it fits into a broader strategic framework.

U.S. Agencies Lack a Common Understanding of Institutional Capacity-Building

As stated at the outset of this report, the DSCA defines *ICB* as "projects that enhance the capacity of partner nations to exercise responsible civilian control of its national security forces, contribute to collective security, and absorb, apply, and sustain national security capabilities."[1] In practice, how-

1 Defense Security Cooperation Agency, "Institutional Capacity Building," undated.

ever, this definition seems to provide little clarity.[2] There are pronounced differences in how different U.S. government agencies think of ICB. DoD personnel typically have a much narrower understanding of what ICB is, using the term to refer to efforts to improve partners' logistics and sustainment capabilities, with less attention to efforts aimed at the higher levels often associated with security sector reform or security governance. In contrast, ICB efforts at DoS often put more emphasis on broader governance concerns (such as military command and control and civil-military relations). In some cases, they engage parties beyond the MoD, such as partners' ministries of justice.[3]

Institutional Capacity-Building Is Rarely Strategically Employed as a Tool of Influence

There is a great deal of disagreement among U.S. practitioners about whether the United States does use ICB as a tool of competition and whether it should. In general, for most U.S. government personnel, the linkages between ICB and influence in competition—to the extent they exist at all—seem to be predominantly implicit.[4]

As was the case with differing definitions of ICB, there were pronounced differences between major agencies about the purpose of ICB. DoD appears to see SSA generally as a tool of strategic competition, with an emphasis on what we have called the resources and relationships pathways to influence. But ICB as a mechanism of influence appears to be devalued in much of DoD (with important exceptions, especially at the embassy level).[5] Several observers noted that ICB is an "afterthought" at AFRICOM, saying that

---

2 Marquis et al., forthcoming.

3 U.S. Department of State, "The Global Defense Reform Program," PowerPoint slides provided to RAND by the Bureau of Political-Military Affairs, March 24, 2021.

4 Observers have made a similar critique of SSA more broadly, asserting that SSA as currently applied fails to meaningfully contribute to strategic competition objectives. See, for example, Stephen Tankel and Tommy Ross, "Retooling U.S. Security Sector Assistance," *War on the Rocks*, October 28, 2020.

5 This devaluation occurs in part because of DoD processes and the manner in which ICB responsibilities are fragmented across a disparate array of actors—a point to which we return below.

the command largely does not appreciate the purpose of ICB programs, nor does it take an active role in promoting ICB with partners.[6] One observer noted that in some partner nations ICB is used as a mechanism to grease the wheels of so-called "Section 333" training-and-equipping packages, and another remarked that ICB is used as "window dressing" or "fairy dust" to justify additional funding for train-and-equip.[7] DoS personnel, on the other hand, are more likely to think in broader terms about the implications of ICB programming, but they typically think about such programs in terms of influence generally rather than strategic competition specifically.

Some of the U.S. government personnel and others interviewed for this study were critical of thinking about ICB through a competition lens, but this was mostly because they believed that the competition concept provoked a "reactive" response in which U.S. ICB efforts were conceived through a zero-sum and short-term mindset.[8] Interviewees with this perspective maintained that that a competition framing will also likely be unattractive to African partners, because most of them prefer to have multiple external security partners as a way of importing more ideas, technology, and capacity.[9] This dynamic may be particularly pronounced in Africa given Cold War histories of great-power rivalry on the continent.

6 RAND interview with former U.S. ambassador in Africa, March 26, 2021 (Interview 3); RAND interview with U.S. government ICB implementer, April 2, 2021 (Interview 2); RAND interview with four U.S. government ICB implementers, March 26, 2021 (Interview 4). There are, of course, important exceptions; some AFRICOM personnel have given considerable thought to ICB.

7 RAND interview with former U.S. ambassador in Africa, March 26, 2021 (Interview 3); RAND interview with U.S. government ICB implementer, April 2, 2021 (Interview 2); RAND interview with Defense Security Cooperation Agency official, March 24, 2021 (Interview 19); RAND interview with U.S. DoD official, April 20, 2021 (Interview 24).

8 RAND interview with three U.S. government Africa subject-matter experts, February 17, 2021 (Interview 12).

9 See for example, Aning and Siegle, 2019.

Successes and Failures of Institutional Capacity-Building as a Tool of Influence in Africa

We can empirically analyze only actions that have been taken, not those that might have been taken had ICB played a more prominent role in U.S. SSA. In examining successes and failures of ICB as a tool of influence in Africa, we are constrained by the United States' actual practice of ICB, with all of the limitations described in the previous section. We cannot with confidence say what a more intensive, holistic U.S. commitment to ICB might yield. We can nonetheless offer a number of initial insights that might help to inform future efforts.

Institutional Capacity-Building Programs Can Be a Moderately Valued Resource for Partners in Africa

Our case studies of Niger and Kenya suggest that ICB programs can offer valuable support to U.S. partners. To the extent U.S. ICB programs make partner-nation security sectors more capable of combating major threats or more efficient in their use of scarce resources, the leaders of those countries are likely to value such programs. This, in turn, offers the potential for increasing U.S. influence in countries eager to continue or expand on such programs.

The potential for influence, however, can be easily overstated. Most African governments have sustained themselves without large-scale SSA or major reforms of their security sectors. They are unlikely to make major sacrifices—including risking offending other potential donor nations or investors, such as China—out of gratitude for U.S. support or a desire to continue such programs. Even a country as aid-dependent as South Sudan was willing to accept enormous amounts of U.S. assistance without a concomitant willingness to undertake reforms the United States requested. As our review of related literature suggested, the provision of valued resources to partner nations can generate some degree of U.S. influence—but normally only modest amounts, and only for so long as U.S. and partner short-term interests are relatively closely aligned.

Efforts to Build Resilience in Partners' Security Sectors Appear to Have Yielded Limited Results

This report has suggested two paths to influence through resilience: (1) building capacity within partner nations' security sectors to resist malign activities by U.S. competitors that directly target the security sector and (2) building capacity more broadly in an effort to make partners stable, prosperous, and well-governed. There is little evidence that China is directly targeting the security sectors of African states other than through arms sales and education programs that present a different model of civil-military relations than the Western model. Consequently, if resilience contributes to U.S. influence goals at all, it is largely through the indirect pathway.

The most impressive achievements of ambitious ICB efforts have been in highly aid-dependent, postconflict countries, such as Liberia and Sierra Leone, in which the governments clearly recognized the need for reform of their security sectors.[10] Under more typical conditions, African governments are generally reluctant to undertake wide-ranging reforms, although they might be more open to narrower, more targeted initiatives. In many ways, the logic behind this reluctance to change is understandable. Many of these countries face serious threats, including subpopulations that are taking (or have in the recent past taken) up arms against the government, the risk of coups, and sometimes threats from beyond their borders. Many leaders face a choice between (1) making do with a security sector that may be highly flawed but appears adequate to the government's needs and (2) seeking major improvements, with a risk of catastrophic failure if they misjudge the consequences of reform.

Especially under conditions of strategic competition, the United States has few negative incentives ("sticks") to motivate reform. Instead, it must rely on persuasion and inducements. This fact highlights the importance of choosing U.S. partners wisely. Among reasonably well-governed states with some commitment to reform, ICB programs might offer incremental

[10] South Sudan was also a postconflict country that enjoyed considerable aid. But its leadership did not perceive drastic reforms of its dysfunctional security sector as being in its interest, and the promise of revenues from the country's hydrocarbon resources may have given the leadership more freedom of action than leaders in Freetown and Monrovia believed they had.

gains in resilience that could, over long periods of time, amount to important contributions to both African partners' and the United States' goals. In other circumstances, ICB has a high risk of being mere "window dressing" to facilitate the transfer of materiel from the United States to partner governments, with little subsequent U.S. influence over how they use those capabilities.

Improved Relationships Through Institutional Capacity-Building Offer Hope for Increasing U.S. Influence, but They Must Be Nurtured

Prior research suggests that interactions between U.S. and partner security personnel can help to build U.S. influence on the basis of trust and shared values. But usually such relationships only form through intensive interactions over extended periods of time. The case studies in this report lend support to this conclusion. ICB programs often engaged senior leaders in partner nations. Some U.S. ICB implementing partners returned to the same country over the course of a half-dozen or more years, allowing them to build on relationships begun and nurtured years before. In Nigeria, the United States partnered with a retired senior Nigerian general to attempt to build the contacts and trust necessary for progress in ICB. Many of the interviewees with whom we spoke—including many with no stake in ICB programs but who had interacted intensively with key figures in African partner nations—said that the United States had gained a not-insignificant amount of goodwill and trust through such programs. Even in cases like South Sudan that can only be considered failures, there was evidence that many of the military officers who had worked most intensively with the United States remained well-disposed to the United States in the years after SSA to Juba was terminated.

What Might Explain Success and Failure?

Across all three pathways to influence—resources, resilience, and relationships—three factors appear conducive to improving U.S. influence with African partner nations.

Partner Commitment to Reform Is Critical

Partner commitment to reform—what is frequently described as "political will"—is a necessary but not sufficient condition for the success of ICB programs, understood immediately in terms of capacity-building and, in the longer term, influence. In both Niger and Kenya, partner-government leaders recognized the need for reforms. In Niger, this commitment encompassed a wide range of defense functions, whereas in Kenya it was limited to much narrower goals. But in both cases, not only did the partner governments make strides in their security capabilities, they also appeared to value the services that the United States offered. In contrast, in Nigeria and South Sudan, not only did partner-nation leaders fail to implement changes recommended by the United States, they frequently resented U.S. pressure for reforms.

There is nothing novel in noting the importance of "political will." Indeed, DoD's assessment, monitoring, and evaluation (AM&E) framework for SSA requires combatant commands to conduct an initial assessment prior to undertaking security cooperation which includes, among other things, "the feasibility of achieving successful outcomes based on a partner's political willingness to pursue the desired outcome."[11] The challenges lie in accurately diagnosing and supporting such commitment to reform. "Will" is neither static nor uniform; in many cases, there will be some partner-nation leaders who embrace change and others who resist it, and the balance of influence between these groups will change over time.

There are mechanisms the United States can employ to help navigate these challenges—a point to which we return in our recommendations in Chapter Five. But it is important to highlight that our research (like that of others[12]) suggests relatively limited appetite among most countries in Africa to allow external actors (including the United States) a major role in addressing such sensitive matters as corruption, the security sector's respect

[11] Department of Defense Instruction 5123.14, *Assessment, Monitoring, and Evaluation Policy for the Security Cooperation Enterprise*, Washington, D.C.: U.S. Department of Defense, January 13, 2017.

[12] For an overview of the challenges involved in reforms among many African militaries, see Herbert M. Howe, *Ambiguous Order: Military Forces in African States*, Boulder, Colo.: Lynne Rienner Publishers, 2001.

for human rights, or civil-military relations.[13] This finding suggests limits to what ICB programs can accomplish and the need to build trust and support constituencies for reform over long periods of time.

Long-Term U.S. Commitment Greatly Improves the Odds of Success

The evidence from prior related studies and from the case studies in this report both suggest the importance of long-term U.S. commitment. Trust- and values-based relationships only form through repeated, long-running interactions. Resilient institutions take time to build. Even U.S. resources tend to be valued more if the partner believes they will continue to be provided into the future. The case studies of both Niger and Kenya highlighted some of these dynamics. One advantage of ICB implementing partners is that they can continue to work with partners on the same set of issues for many years—much longer than a typical U.S. embassy tour. On the other hand, long-term engagement is no guarantee of success, as the Nigeria case suggests.

In-Country Presence Is Required to Deepen Relationships and Sustain Momentum

Several of the people interviewed for this study noted that progress—both at a programmatic level and in terms of building strong relationships—tended to stall when personnel responsible for ICB programs were not in-country. In contrast, in countries such as Niger—where the United States had a well-respected, senior-level ICB coordinator continuously on the ground, actively working the project portfolio with partners—progress tended to be more consistent. A model in which a former senior U.S. government official (such as a former ambassador with knowledge of the region) is contracted as an implementing partner may be particularly effective. Such personnel can

[13] There are certainly exceptions—particularly in postconflict societies, such as Liberia or Sierra Leone, that recognize their dependence on external actors to overhaul their security sectors. Other African countries, such as post-apartheid South Africa, have embraced the need for reforms, even if they have not allowed external actors to play a major role in them.

provide both continuity and visibility to ICB efforts. However, interviewees also emphasized that U.S. embassy personnel with responsibilities for SSA would benefit from improved training and guidance on how to meaningfully integrate ICB into SSA initiatives.[14]

---

[14] RAND interview with DoD official, April 20, 2021 (Interview 24).

CHAPTER FIVE

Recommendations

In this report, we examined U.S. ICB programs for the security sectors of African partner governments and their potential role in strategic competition, particularly with China. We have shown that ICB, if done right under the right conditions, can pay dividends as a tool of influence, although largely in support of a broader U.S. approach. In this concluding section, we outline initial recommendations for how U.S. SSA policy could better integrate its governance and competition objectives in Africa, starting at the strategic level and moving to more specific practices.

Overarching Recommendations

Prioritize Resilience—but with Modest Expectations About U.S. Impact

Without resilient security sectors that remain committed to protecting their states and populations as a whole, all other pathways to U.S. influence among its African partners can founder, as the example of South Sudan suggests. On the other hand, we found only limited evidence that external ICB programs have contributed to resilience in Africa outside of certain post-conflict contexts (such as Sierra Leone and Liberia). Moreover, there is some risk to the United States' future influence when it presses for reforms that partners are unwilling to embrace, as the Nigeria and South Sudan cases suggest.

How, then, should the United States balance the need for resilience with a recognition that U.S. efforts will typically contribute only incrementally toward this goal? The overarching lesson appears to be that resilience concerns (and the broader security governance it represents) should inform all

U.S. ICB planning. Where possible, the United States should strive to make incremental gains. Where such gains appear unlikely, the United States should strongly consider whether sizable SSA commitments are appropriate, especially given the risks of blowback if U.S. support is misused by partner nations.[1]

These considerations are particularly important in the United States' strategic shift to competition, as arguments for overlooking anti-democratic, abusive behavior of partners that receive SSA or purchase weapons from the United States might become more prominent for fear of ceding ground to U.S. competitors. As some of our interviewees noted, the United States' democratic model provides a powerful comparative advantage and aligns well with the aspirations of ordinary citizens and security sector officials in many African partner nations.[2] The United States should thus avoid an SSA "race to the bottom" with China or other competitors.

Embed the Provision of Security Resources Within More Comprehensive Planning Efforts

Resources can be helpful in gaining influence, but only if embedded in a broader and longer-term political-military plan that incorporates resilience and relationships. Equipment that does not serve a long-term purpose is not only wasted but can actively harm U.S. influence, as a number of episodes in the U.S.-Nigeria relationship demonstrate. Some progress has been made on this front—such as the development of Significant Security Cooperation Initiatives (SSCIs). But there is room for considerable improvement, particularly given concerns that the SSCI process might simply be used as a vehicle to push predetermined train-and-equip packages rather than a comprehensive plan informed by a country-specific theory of change.[3]

---

1 As indicated in the section below on specific practices, a mechanism like the Millennium Challenge Corporation might help to differentiate in which countries gains to resilience appear most likely.

2 RAND interview with three U.S. government Africa subject-matter experts, February 17, 2021 (Interview 12); Robert Mattes, "Democracy in Africa: Demand, Supply, and the 'Dissatisfied Democrat,'" Afrobarometer Policy Paper No. 54, February 2019.

3 An array of legislative and bureaucratic hurdles present challenges to holistic, long-term planning remain, including congressional appropriations cycles, legislative author-

Where possible, the U.S. government should establish specific mechanisms that permit longer-term planning (a number of which are outlined in more detail below). Where this is not possible, U.S. agencies should still make every effort within existing planning processes (such as Country Security Cooperation Plans, Integrated Country Strategies, and Theater Campaign Plans) to emphasize longer-term, more holistic efforts. In particular, the Office of the Under Secretary of Defense for Policy (both regional and functional offices) has a critical role to play in ensuring an appropriate balance between U.S. strategic competition, governance, and capability objectives.

Recommendations for Specific Practices

Translating these broad principles into policy can be facilitated through five more specific practices.

Codify and Actively Socialize a Common Understanding of Institutional Capacity-Building Across the U.S. Government

The U.S. government should establish guidance defining ICB in order to set the stage for a systematic, coordinated approach to ICB across the interagency. As we noted earlier, there is no clear understanding of what comprises ICB, what it should be used for, and how it fits into the United States' broader foreign policy toolkit. Much of the confusion surrounding ICB stems from the lack of policy guidance on ICB and a clear definition. We recommend that ICB stakeholders across the U.S. government codify ICB practice in policy and doctrine, such as in the form of a Presidential Policy Directive, which in turn would inform the development of a DoD Instruction and/or a joint publication with DoS and other stakeholders. A common understanding of ICB and what it is meant to achieve will drive an

ities tied to very specific functions (often counterterrorism) that do not match priority strategic needs, legacy commitments, and high personnel turnover rates in many parts of the U.S. SSA enterprise. Nonetheless, some limitations are self-inflicted, including a tendency to prioritize immediate perceived threats over long-term relationships.

informed analysis of ICB activities for purposes of prioritization, planning, and AM&E.

Strengthen Interagency Coordination Via a Security Sector Assistance Hub

The United States should aim to better integrate and coordinate U.S. government efforts to maintain influence with efforts to build partner militaries' capabilities in an accountable, sustainable manner. To help the U.S. government achieve a common understanding of how ICB might contribute to these two objectives—and better plan and coordinate ICB with other SSA efforts—the U.S. government could strengthen existing interagency coordination mechanisms and working groups through an interagency SSA hub or "council."[4] The body would coordinate existing integration efforts and serve as a clearinghouse for all SSA and ICB programs (Title 10 and Title 22), including how to integrate influence and governance goals on a case-by-case basis. It would meet quarterly and be overseen by the National Security Council but would be co-chaired by officials from the Office of the Secretary of Defense at DoD and the Political Military Bureau at DoS, with representatives from other relevant stakeholders, including the U.S. Agency for International Development, the U.S. Department of Justice, the U.S. Department of Homeland Security, and others.

Incentivize Partner Commitment to Institutional Reforms Through Selective, Graduated Security Sector Assistance

The interagency hub should also stand up a graduated SSA pilot program along the lines of the Millennium Challenge Corporation (MCC). Scholars and practitioners have previously recommended similar initiatives, as did many officials interviewed for this study.[5] An MCC-like mechanism for

---

[4] This proposal, along with the one for a DoD Instruction, align with similar recommendation made by Marquis et al., forthcoming, p. 73.

[5] For example, see United States Institute of Peace, Task Force on Extremism in Fragile States, *Preventing Extremism in Fragile States, A New Approach*, February 2019,

SSA, whereby SSA providers and recipients work together to identify a package of shared objectives and clear expectations for achieving them over a five- to ten-year period, would enable longer-term planning and continuity in programming while incentivizing partners to undertake potentially difficult institutional reforms sought by ICB programs.

The program could adopt MCC's most successful features, including non-earmarked funding, recipient design and ownership, grants-based financing, time-limited projects, and transparent eligibility criteria. The United States could establish memoranda of understanding (MoUs) with countries that meet the criteria and express interest in pursuing the partnership. Milestones established in the MoU—such as reducing corruption, improving adherence to human rights, and other security reforms—should be built into the agreement such that when a partner meets the agreed-upon milestone, it "unlocks" the agreed-upon assistance. As a partner achieves key milestones, it will also be able to "graduate" into a new status that allows increased access to different quantities and types of U.S. assistance, or even other diplomatic benefits.[6] If the partner reneges on the conditions outlined in the MoU, there would be a suspension or redirection of funds to other participating countries or candidates. The initiative would be housed at DoS with robust engagement from DoD and other SSA stakeholders. Congress should authorize this pilot initiative with a separate pot of dedicated funding.[7]

---

pp. 50–53; Tommy Ross and Melissa Dalton, "A Roadmap for Better Choices from Security Partners," *War on the Rocks*, January 17, 2020; Melissa Dalton, Hijab Shah, Shannon N. Green, and Rebecca Hughes, *Oversight and Accountability in U.S. Security Sector Assistance: Seeking Return on Investment*, Washington, D.C.: Center for Strategic and International Studies, February 2018; Gordon Adams and Richard Sokolsky, "Governance and Security Sector Assistance: The Missing Link—Part II," *Lawfare*, July 19, 2015; Stephen Tankel and Melissa Dalton, "How to Improve Return on Investment for Security Assistance," *Lawfare*, August 27, 2017; Max Bergmann and Alexandra Schmitt, *A Plan to Reform U.S. Security Assistance*, Washington, D.C.: Center for American Progress, March 9, 2021.

[6] United States Institute of Peace, Task Force on Extremism in Fragile States, 2019.

[7] Congress would have to authorize the program, and each administration would need to develop funding requests for Congress that match the compacts established for each country and request that Congress fund a line-item budget allocation for the duration of the compact.

Such a model would help reveal where true alignment exists in partnerships, reward action with real resources, and build lasting relationships that would be more likely to pay dividends along all three influence pathways discussed in this study. In particular, it would enable the United States to better elevate resilience considerations with potentially risky partners, as it would establish incentives, clear redlines, and offramps in SSA relationships.

Build Relationships Through Long-Term Commitments and Intensive In-Country Cooperation

Relationships are built over long periods of time and through frequent and repeated interaction. The United States might advance these objectives through the following practices:

- committing to longer tours and/or more civilian personnel at AFRICOM headquarters and ensuring that headquarters personnel play an active role in maintaining relationships with partners on the continent
- committing additional resources to programs, such as a U.S. Ministry of Defense Advisor and the Global Defense Reform Program, to establish U.S. personnel as embedded advisors in key partners who support such positions
- where warranted, using the same nongovernmental implementing partners over many years
- making greater use of U.S. organizations and programs that emphasize continuity, including the State Partnership Program and the National Defense University's Africa Center for Strategic Studies
- coordinating ICB efforts with allies who may have deeper relationships and greater influence with partner officials at the ministerial levels.

Redouble Assessment, Monitoring, and Evaluation Efforts

In the end, effectively using ICB to advance U.S. competition objectives will require a better understanding of "what works" in this field. We have provided evidence from related fields and we have used case studies to suggest that these prior findings are relevant to the use of ICB in the current context in Africa. But such an approach does not substitute for the rigorous collection and evaluation of data over time.

DoD has made substantial progress in recent years in establishing and implementing a nascent AM&E framework for security cooperation.[8] DoS is in the process of developing a similar framework for Title 22 security assistance, which includes both security governance and influence as specific outcomes of DoS SSA.[9] These initiatives are a welcome step toward systematic evaluations of SSA's effectiveness, but obstacles remain, including poor data collection and dissemination, vaguely defined objectives, and resistance in some parts of the enterprise to new AM&E processes. ICB is particularly difficult to evaluate, with many U.S. programs in their infancy and the outcomes of ICB (changes in institutions) requiring consistent measurement over a long time horizon. Data on ICB are sparse, limiting the ability of the U.S. government to understand the landscape of activities, how they are being leveraged, and whether they have effects relevant to competition.[10]

DoD and DoS should redouble efforts to implement rigorous AM&E for U.S. SSA and further apply an AM&E framework to ICB programs. The aforementioned ICB board should, at minimum, provide reporting and tracking requirements for ICB planners and implementers. In addition, DoD could include more ICB programs, such as VILA or SGI, on its strategic evaluation agenda.[11]

---

8 The FY2017 NDAA required DoD to develop a standardized, objective evaluation of its security cooperation initiatives; following the enactment of FY2017 NDAA, DoD issued DoD Instruction 5123.14 establishing its AM&E policy for security cooperation and identified the roles and responsibilities for relevant DoD components. DoD now requires initial assessments of partner's willingness to implement and sustain assistance, theories of change for security cooperation, performance monitoring, and evaluations.

9 U.S. Department of State, Bureau of Political-Military Affairs, "Strategic Planning & The PM Evaluation Framework," April 2021b, not available to the general public.

10 Much of the evidence on the outcomes of ICB is confined to after-action reviews of DoD implementers, or anecdotes derived from interviews. A forthcoming RAND study on U.S. ICB activities managed by DSCA was unable to verify whether a substantial portion of activities labeled as ICB were actually ICB because of scant and/or inconsistent descriptions (Marquis et al., forthcoming, p. 21).

11 Evaluations of ICB in Indonesia and Colombia are currently underway.

Although not without risks, ICB can play a key role in integrating and achieving the dual U.S. strategic objectives of competition and improved governance in Africa. This report helps provide a template for how the U.S. government could rethink SSA policies to do so.

APPENDIX

Interview Descriptions

Table provides the dates of the interviews we conducted for this research and brief descriptions of the interviewees.

TABLE A.1
Interview Descriptions

Number	Identifier	Date
1	Two U.S. government ICB implementers	2-Feb-21
2	U.S. government ICB implementer	2-Apr-21
3	Former U.S. ambassador in Africa	26-Mar-21
4	Four U.S. government ICB implementers	26-Mar-21
5	Former U.S. defense attaché in Africa	5-Mar-21
6	Former U.S. official with previous responsibilities for Nigeria	22-Mar-21
7	U.S. government ICB implementer	17-Mar-21
8	Former U.S. government ICB implementer	12-Mar-21
9	Two U.S. government Africa subject-matter experts	23-Mar-21
10	U.S. embassy official	16-Apr-21
11	Two nongovernment Africa subject-matter experts	11-Feb-21
12	Three U.S. government Africa subject-matter experts	17-Feb-21
13	Former U.S. government ICB implementer	5-Apr-21
14	Former U.S. ambassador in Kenya	2-Mar-21
15	Former Kenyan military official	5-Mar-21

TABLE A.1—CONTINUED

Number	Identifier	Date
16	U.S. State Department official with previous responsibilities for South Sudan and Kenya	18-Feb-21
17	U.S. State Department official with previous responsibilities for South Sudan	12-Feb-21
18	Former South Sudanese government official	25-Feb-21
19	Defense Security Cooperation Agency official	24-Mar-21
20	Two U.S. government ICB implementers	17-Feb-21
21	U.S. State Department official with previous responsibilities for South Sudan	12-Feb-21
22	U.S. defense attaché with multiple tours in Africa	25-Feb-21
23	U.S. government expert in African affairs	25-Feb-21
24	DoD official	20-April-21
25	Nongovernment Africa subject-matter expert	24-April-21

Abbreviations

AM&E	assessment, monitoring, and evaluation
AMEP	African Military Education Partnership
AMISOM	African Union Mission in Somalia
CRS	Congressional Research Service
DIB	defense institution building
DoD	U.S. Department of Defense
DoS	U.S. Department of State
DSCA	Defense Security Cooperation Agency
ICB	institutional capacity building
IMET	International Military Exchange and Training
ISG	Institute for Security Governance
KDF	Kenyan Defense Forces
MoD	Ministry of Defense
MoI	Ministry of Interior
MoU	memorandum of understanding
MNJTF	Multinational Joint Task Force
NDAA	National Defense Authorization Act
PLA	People's Liberation Army
PME	professional military education
SGI	Security Governance Initiative
SPLA	Sudan People's Liberation Army
SPLM	Sudan People's Liberation Movement
SSA	security sector assistance
VILA	Vertically Integrated Logistics Approach

References

Acker, Kevin, and Deborah Brautigam, *Twenty Years of Data on China's Africa Lending*, Johns Hopkins School of Advanced International Studies, China Africa Research Initiative, 2021.

Adams, Gordon and Richard Sokolsky, "Governance and Security Sector Assistance: The Missing Link—Part II," *Lawfare*, July 19, 2015.

Albert, Eleanor, "China in Africa," Council on Foreign Relations, July 12, 2017.

Anderson, Eva, and Matthew T. Page, *Weaponising Transparency: Defense Procurement Reform as a Counterterrorism Strategy in Nigeria*, Transparency International, May 2017.

Aning, Kwesi, and Joseph Siegle, *Assessing Attitudes of the Next Generation of African Security Sector Professionals*, Africa Center for Strategic Studies, May 1, 2019.

Arieff, Alexis, "U.S. Counterterrorism Priorities and Challenges in Africa," statement before the Committee on Oversight and Reform, Subcommittee on National Security, U.S. House of Representatives, December 16, 2019.

Arieff, Alexis, Kathleen J. McInnis, Lauren Ploch Blanchard, John W. Rollins, Andrew Feickert, and Matthew C. Weed, *Niger: Frequently Asked Questions About the October 2017 Attack on U.S. Soldiers*, Washington, D.C.: Congressional Research Service, RR44995, October 27, 2017.

Ashford, Emma, "Great-Power Competition Is a Recipe for Disaster," *Foreign Policy*, April 1, 2021.

Atkinson, Carol, "Constructivist Implications of Material Power: Military Engagement and the Socialization of States, 1972–2000," *International Studies Quarterly*, Vol. 50, 2006, pp. 509–537.

Bearak, Max, "In Strategic Djibouti, a Microcosm of China's Growing Foothold in Africa," *Washington Post*, December 30, 2019.

Bergmann, Max, and Alexandra Schmitt, *A Plan to Reform U.S. Security Assistance*, Washington, D.C.: Center for American Progress, March 9, 2021.

Bermeo, Sarah Blodgett, "Aid Is Not Oil: Donor Utility, Heterogeneous Aid, and the Aid-Democratization Relationship," *International Organization*, Vol. 70, No. 1, Winter 2016, pp. 1–32.

Berschinski, Robert G., *AFRICOM's Dilemma: The "Global War on Terrorism," "Capacity Building," Humanitarianism, and the Future of U.S. Security Policy in Africa*, Carlisle Barracks, Pa.: Strategic Studies Institute, U.S. Army War College, 2007.

Biden, Joseph R., Jr., *Interim National Security Strategic Guidance*, Washington, D.C.: The White House, March 2021.

Blanchard, Lauren Ploch, *Kenya*, Washington, D.C.: Congressional Research Service, IF10168, 2020.

Blankenship, Brian, and Renanah Miles Joyce, "Purchasing Power: U.S. Overseas Defense Spending and Military Statecraft," *Journal of Conflict Resolution*, Vol. 64, Nos. 2–3, 2020, pp. 545–573.

Boutton, Andrew, "U.S. Foreign Aid, Interstate Rivalry, and Incentives for Counterterrorism Cooperation," *Journal of Peace Research*, Vol. 51, No. 6, 2014, pp. 741–754.

Brautigam, Deborah, and Meg Rithmire, "The Chinese 'Debt Trap' Is a Myth," *The Atlantic*, February 6, 2021.

Brautigam, Deborah, and Won Kidane, *China, Africa, and Debt Distress: Fact and Fiction About Asset Seizures*, Johns Hopkins China Africa Research Initiative Policy Brief No. 47, 2020.

Chalfin, Julie E., and Linda Thomas Greenfield, "The Security Governance Initiative," *PRISM*, May 2017.

Congressional Research Service, *Nigeria: Current Issues and U.S. Policy*, Washington, D.C., RL33964, updated September 18, 2020.

Conley, Heather A., *Russian Malign Influence in Montenegro: The Weaponization and Exploitation of History, Religion, and Economics*, Washington, D.C.: Center for Strategic and International Studies, 2019.

Copeland, Casie, *Dancing in the Dark: Divergent Approaches to Improving Security and Justice in South Sudan*, The Hague: Clingendael Institute, 2015.

Custer, S., M. DiLorenzo, T. Masaki, T. Sethi, and A. Harutyunyan, *Listening to Leaders 2018: Is Development Cooperation Tuned-In or Tone-Deaf?* Williamsburg, Va.: AidData at the College of William & Mary, 2018.

Dalton, Melissa, Hijab Shah, Shannon N. Green, and Rebecca Hughes, *Oversight and Accountability in U.S. Security Sector Assistance: Seeking Return on Investment*, Washington, D.C., Center for Strategic and International Studies, February 2018.

Davis, Robert, Nicole Henderson, and Cybele Merrick, "Community Policing: Variations on the Western Model in the Developing World," *Police Practice and Research*, Vol. 4, No. 3, 2003.

Defense Institute of International Legal Studies, *Annual Report*, 2011.

Defense Institute of International Legal Studies, *Annual Report*, 2014.

Defense Institute of International Legal Studies, *Annual Report*, 2015.

Defense Institute of International Legal Studies, *Annual Report*, 2016.

Defense Institute of International Legal Studies, *Annual Report*, 2017.

Defense Security Cooperation Agency, "Institutional Capacity Building," undated. As of March 15, 2021:
https://www.dsca.mil/institutional-capacity-building

Department of Defense Instruction 5123.14, *Assessment, Monitoring, and Evaluation Policy for the Security Cooperation Enterprise*, Washington, D.C.: U.S. Department of Defense, January 13, 2017.

Dollar, David, *Understanding China's Belt and Road Infrastructure Projects in Africa*, Washington, D.C.: Brookings Institution, September 2019.

Dreher, Axel, Peter Nunnenkamp, and Rainer Thiele, "Does U.S. Aid Buy UN General Assembly Votes? A Disaggregated Analysis," *Public Choice*, Vol. 136, 2008, pp. 139–164.

Finkel, Steven E., Anibal Perez-Liñan, and Mitchell A. Seligson, "The Effects of U.S. Foreign Assistance on Democracy Building, 1990–2003," *World Politics*, Vol. 59, No.3, April 2007, pp. 404–440.

Friend, Alice Hunt, *Civilian Protection Through Civilian Control: An Overlooked Piece of Security Sector Assistance in the Sahel*, Washington, D.C.: Center for Strategic and International Studies, 2020.

Gates, Robert M., "Remarks as Delivered by Secretary of Defense Robert M. Gates at the Nixon Center," Washington, D.C., February 24, 2010.

Gheciu, Alexandra, "Security Institutions as Agents of Socialization? NATO and the 'New Europe,'" *International Organization*, Vol. 59, Fall 2005.

Gilchrist, Narrelle, and Norman Eisen, *Corruption and Terrorism: The Case of Kenya*, Washington, D.C.: Brookings Institution, 2019.

Goldfarb, Zachary A., "U.S., Djibouti Reach Agreement to Keep Counterterrorism Base in Horn of Africa Nation," *Washington Post*, May 5, 2014.

"Half of Vehicles Delivered to Nigerian Army by US Govt Faulty," Legit, January 8, 2016.

Hanlon, Querine, and Richard Shultz, *Prioritizing Security Sector Reform: A New U.S. Approach*, Washington, D.C.: United States Institute of Peace, 2016.

Harkavy, Robert E., *Bases Abroad: The Global Foreign Military Presence*, New York: Oxford University Press for the Stockholm International Peace Research Institute, 1989.

Heath, Timothy R., Derek Grossman, and Asha Clark, *China's Quest for Global Primacy: An Analysis of Chinese International and Defense Strategies to Outcompete the United States*, Santa Monica, Calif.: RAND Corporation, RR-A447-1, 2021. As of September 14, 2021:
https://www.rand.org/pubs/research_reports/RRA447-1.html

Hosenball, Mark, "Human Rights Concerns Limit U.S. Intelligence, Military Aid to Nigeria," Reuters, March 13, 2015.

Howe, Herbert M., *Ambiguous Order: Military Forces in African States*, Boulder, Colo.: Lynne Rienner Publishers, 2001.

Husted, Tomas F., Alexis Arieff, Lauren Ploch Blanchard, and Nicolas Cook, *U.S. Assistance to Sub-Saharan Africa: An Overview*, Washington, D.C.: Congressional Research Service, R46368, May 20, 2020.

International Crisis Group, *Nigeria: The Challenge of Military Reform*, June 6, 2016.

International Crisis Group, *China's Foreign Policy Experiment in South Sudan*, July 2017.

International Monetary Fund, African Department, *A Rebalancing Act for China and Africa: The Effects of China's Rebalancing on Sub-Saharan Africa's Trade and Growth*, April 2017.

Johns Hopkins School of Advanced International Studies, China Africa Research Initiative, "Data: Chinese Global Foreign Aid," webpage, 2021a. As of September 14, 2021:
http://www.sais-cari.org/data-chinese-global-foreign-aid

Johns Hopkins School of Advanced International Studies, China Africa Research Initiative, "Data: Chinese Investment in Africa," webpage, 2021b. As of October 21, 2021:
http://www.sais-cari.org/chinese-investment-in-africa

Jowell, Marco, "The Unintended Consequences of Foreign Military Assistance in Africa: An Analysis of Peacekeeping Training in Kenya," *Journal of Eastern African Studies*, Vol. 12, No. 1, 2018, pp. 102–119.

Joyce, Renanah Miles, "Mixed Messages: Foreign Military Training and Conflict Between Liberal Norms," unpublished manuscript, January 31, 2021.

Lefebvre, Jefferey A., *Arms for the Horn: U.S. Security Policy in Ethiopia and Somalia, 1953–1991*, Pittsburgh, Pa.: University of Pittsburgh Press, 1991.

Levitsky, Steven, and Lucan A. Way, "Linkage Versus Leverage: Rethinking the International Dimension of Regime Change," *Comparative Politics*, Vol. 38, No. 4, July 2006, pp. 379–400.

Machain, Carla Martinez, "Exporting Influence: U.S. Military Training as Soft Power," *Journal of Conflict Resolution*, Vol. 65, Nos. 2–3, 2020, pp. 313–341.

MacLachlan, Karolina, *Corruption as Statecraft: Using Corrupt Practices as Foreign Policy Tools*, Transparency International—Defense and Security, 2019.

Marquis, Jefferson P., David Thaler, Jennifer D.P. Moroney, Beth Grill, Mary Kate Adgie, and Alexander Noyes, *Department of Defense Institutional Capacity-Building of Foreign Partner Security Forces: An Approach to Analyzing Potential Gaps Between Supply and Demand*, Santa Monica, Calif.: RAND Corporation, forthcoming.

Matisek, Jahara, "International Competition to Provide Security Force Assistance in Africa: Civil-Military Relations Matter," *PRISM*, Vol. 9, No. 1, 2020.

Mattes, Robert, "Democracy in Africa: Demand, Supply, and the 'Dissatisfied Democrat,'" Afrobarometer Policy Paper No. 54, February 2019.

McNerney, Michael J., Angela O'Mahony, Thomas S. Szayna, Derek Eaton, Caroline Baxter, Colin P. Clarke, Emma Cutrufello, Michael McGee, Heather Peterson, Leslie Adrienne Payne, and Calin Trenkov-Wermuth, *Assessing Security Cooperation as a Preventive Tool*, Santa Monica, Calif.: RAND Corporation, RR-350-A, 2014. As of September 13, 2021: https://www.rand.org/pubs/research_reports/RR350.html

McNerney, Michael J., Stuart Johnson, Stephanie Pezard, David Stebbins, Renanah Miles, Angela O'Mahony, Chaoling Feng, and Tim Oliver, *Defense Institution Building in Africa: An Assessment*, Santa Monica, Calif.: RAND Corporation, RR-1232-OSD, 2016. As of September 13, 2021: https://www.rand.org/pubs/research_reports/RR1232.html

Millennium Challenge Corporation, "Where We Work," undated, accessed April 15, 2021. As of September 13, 2021: https://www.mcc.gov/where-we-work

Nantulya, Paul, "China's Strategic Aims in Africa," testimony before the U.S.-China Economic and Security Review Commission Hearing, May 8, 2020.

Nantulya, Paul, "Reshaping African Agency in China-Africa Relations," Africa Center for Strategic Studies, March 2, 2021.

Neese-Bybee, Ashley, Paul Clarke, and Alexander Noyes, "Defense Institution Building in Africa," *Parameters*, Vol. 50, No. 1, Spring 2020.

"Niger: Attack on Presidential Palace an 'Attempted Coup,'" *Al Jazeera*, March 31, 2021.

O'Grady, Siobhan, "Nigeria to Washington: Take Your Military Aid and Shove It," *Foreign Policy*, December 2, 2014.

Page, Matthew T., *Camouflaged Cash: How "Security Votes" Fuel Corruption in Nigeria*, Transparency International, May 2018a.

Page, Matthew T., *The Intersection of China's Commercial Interests and Nigeria's Conflict Landscape*, Washington, D.C.: United States Institute of Peace, Special Report No. 428, September 2018b.

Pettyjohn, Stacie L., and Jennifer Kavanagh, *Access Granted: Political Challenges to the U.S. Overseas Military Presence, 1945–2014*, Santa Monica, Calif. RAND Corporation, RR-1339-AF, 2016. As of September 13, 2021: https://www.rand.org/pubs/research_reports/RR1339.html

Public Law 114–328, National Defense Authorization Act for Fiscal Year 2017, December 23, 2016.

Rands, Richard, "In Need of Review: SPLA Transformation in 2006–10 and Beyond," *Small Arms Survey*, Graduate Institute of International and Development Studies, Geneva, 2010.

Ratner, Ely, "Reaping What You Sow: Democratic Transitions and Foreign Policy Realignment," *Journal of Conflict Resolution*, Vol. 53, No. 3, June 2009, pp. 390–418.

Ross, Thomas W., "Enhancing Security Cooperation Effectiveness: A Model for Capability Package Planning," *Joint Force Quarterly*, Vol. 80, 1st quarter 2016, pp. 25–34.

Ross, Tommy, and Melissa Dalton, "A Roadmap for Better Choices from Security Partners," *War on the Rocks*, January 17, 2020.

Ruby, Tomislav Z., and Douglas Gibler, "U.S. Professional Military Education and Democratization Abroad," *European Journal of International Relations*, Vol. 16, No. 3, 2010, pp. 339–364.

Sacks, David, "Countries in China's Belt and Road Initiative: Who's in and Who's out," Council on Foreign Relations, March 24, 2021.

Savage, Jesse Dillon, and Jonathan Caverley, "When Human Capital Threatens the Capitol: Foreign Aid in the Form of Military Training and Coups," *Journal of Peace Research*, Vol. 54, No. 4, 2017.

Scobell, Andrew, Bonny Lin, Howard J. Shatz, Michael Johnson, Larry Hanauer, Michael S. Chase, Astrid Stuth Cevallos, Ivan W. Rasmussen, Arthur Chan, Aaron Strong, Eric Warner, and Logan Ma, *At the Dawn of the Belt and Road: China in the Developing World*, Santa Monica, Calif.: RAND Corporation, RR-2273-A, 2018. As of September 13, 2021: https://www.rand.org/pubs/research_reports/RR2273.html

Security Assistance Monitor, "Foreign Military Training: Kenya," accessed April 1, 2021a.

Security Assistance Monitor, website, 2021. As of October 21, 2021: https://securityassistance.org/

Selormey, Edem, "Africans' Perceptions About China: A Sneak Peek from 18 Countries," Afrobarometer, September 3, 2020. As of March 16, 2021: https://afrobarometer.org/sites/default/files/africa-china_relations-3sept20.pdf

Shambaugh, David L., *China Goes Global: The Partial Power*, Oxford: Oxford University Press, 2013.

Shurkin, Michael, "The Good and Bad of the Trump Administration's New Africa Strategy," *The Hill*, December 20, 2018.

Siollun, Max, "No Helicopters for You," *Foreign Policy*, February 3, 2014.

Solomon, Salem, and Casey Frechette, "Corruption Is Wasting Chinese Money in Africa," *Foreign Policy*, September 13, 2018.

State Council Information Office of the People's Republic of China, *China's Military Strategy*, May 2015.

Sullivan, Patricia L., Brock F. Tessman, and Xiaojun Li, "U.S. Military Aid and Recipient State Cooperation," *Foreign Policy Analysis*, Vol. 7, 2011, pp. 275–294.

Tankel, Stephen, and Melissa Dalton, "How to Improve Return on Investment for Security Assistance," *Lawfare*, August 27, 2017.

Tankel, Stephen, and Tommy Ross, "Retooling U.S. Security Sector Assistance," *War on the Rocks*, October 28, 2020.

Tillerson, Rex W., remarks, George Mason University, Fairfax, Va., March 6, 2018.

Townsend, Stephen J., "A Secure and Stable Africa Is an Enduring American Interest," statement before the Senate Armed Service Committee, January 30, 2020.

United States Institute of Peace, Task Force on Extremism in Fragile States, *Preventing Extremism in Fragile States, A New Approach*, February 2019.

U.S. Africa Command, *Institutional Capacity Support Plans*, June 18, 2020, not available to the general public.

U.S. Department of Defense, *Summary of the 2018 National Defense Strategy of the United States of America*, Washington, D.C., 2018. As of September 13, 2021:
https://dod.defense.gov/Portals/1/Documents/pubs/2018-National-Defense-Strategy-Summary.pdf

U.S. Department of Defense, Office of the Inspector General, *Evaluation of Department of Defense Efforts to Build Counterterrorism and Stability Operations Capacity of Foreign Military Forces with Section 1206/2282 Funding*, Washington, D.C., DODIG-2017-099_1206, July 2017.

U.S. Department of State, "2019 Investment Climate Statements: Niger," undated. As of September 13, 2021:
https://www.state.gov/reports/2019-investment-climate-statements/niger/

U.S. Department of State, *Security Governance Initiative: 2017 Review*, Washington, D.C., 2017.

U.S. Department of State, *Security Governance Initiative: Annual Review 2018*, Washington, D.C., 2018.

U.S. Department of State, "Trans-Sahara Counterterrorism Partnership (TSCTP)," February 14, 2019. As of September 13, 2021: https://www.state.gov/trans-sahara-counterterrorism-partnership/

U.S. Department of State, "The Global Defense Reform Program," PowerPoint slides provided to RAND by the Bureau of Political-Military Affairs, March 24, 2021.

U.S. Department of State, Bureau of Political-Military Affairs, "U.S. Security Cooperation with Nigeria," March 19, 2021a. As of September 13, 2021: https://www.state.gov/u-s-security-cooperation-with-nigeria/

U.S. Department of State, Bureau of Political-Military Affairs, "Strategic Planning & The PM Evaluation Framework," April 2021b, not available to the general public.

U.S. House of Representatives, *Joint Explanatory Statement of the Committee of Conference for the Fiscal Year 2017 National Defense Authorization Act*, Washington, D.C.: U.S. Government Printing Office, 2016.

U.S. Senate, "The Nigerian Transition and the Future of U.S. Policy," hearing before the Committee on Foreign Relations, November 4, 1999. As of September 13, 2021: https://www.govinfo.gov/content/pkg/CHRG-106shrg61867/html/CHRG-106shrg61867.htm

Van Oudenaren, John S., and Benjamin E. Fisher, "Foreign Military Education as PLA Soft Power," *Parameters*, Vol. 46, No. 4, Winter 2016, pp. 105–118.

Wang, T. Y., "U.S. Foreign Aid and UN Voting: An Analysis of Important Issues," *International Studies Quarterly*, Vol. 43, No. 1, 1999, pp. 199–210.

Warner, Lesley Anne, "The Disintegration of the Military Integration Process in South Sudan (2006–2013)," *Stability: International Journal of Security and Development*, Vol. 5, No. 1, 2016.

Watts, Stephen, Kimberly Jackson, Sean Mann, and Stephen Dalzell, *A Developmental Approach to Building Sustainable Security-Sector Capacity in Africa*, Santa Monica, Calif.: RAND Corporation, RR-2048-AFRICOM, 2018. As of September 13, 2021: https://www.rand.org/pubs/research_reports/RR2048.html

Watts, Stephen, Trevor Johnston, Matthew Lane, Sean Mann, Michael J. McNerney, and Andrew Brooks, *Building Security in Africa: An Evaluation of U.S. Security Sector Assistance in Africa from the Cold War to the Present*, Santa Monica, Calif.: RAND Corporation, RR-2447-OSD, 2018. As of September 13, 2021: https://www.rand.org/pubs/research_reports/RR2447.html

Wezeman, Pieter D., Aude Fleurant, Alexandra Kuimova, Nan Tian, and Siemon T. Wezeman, *Trends in International Arms Transfers, 2018*, Stockholm International Peace Research Institute, March 2019.

Wezeman, Pieter D., Alexandra Kuimoca, and Siemon T. Wezeman, *Trends in International Arms Transfers, 2020*, Stockholm International Peace Research Institute, March 21, 2020.

The White House, "Fact Sheet: U.S. Security Sector Assistance Policy," Presidential Policy Directive 23, April 5, 2013.

The White House, "Fact Sheet: Security Governance Initiative," August 6, 2014. As of September 13, 2021: https://obamawhitehouse.archives.gov/the-press-office/2014/08/06/fact-sheet-security-governance-initiative